AF539877

MICRO-FINANCE AND SELF-HELP GROUPS

MICRO-FINANCE AND SELF-HELP GROUPS

By

Dr. M. Edwin Gnanadhas

Dr. M. Edwin Gnanadhas
Reader in Commerce
Post Graduate and Research Centre,
Scott Christian College
Nagercoil-629003

M. Mahalekshmi

S.G. Lecturer in Commerce
Sree Devi Kumari Women's College
Kurhithurai

DISCOVERY PUBLISHING HOUSE PVT. LTD.

NEW DELHI-110 002

Published by:
Tilak Wasan

DISCOVERY PUBLISHING HOUSE PVT. LTD.
4831/24, Prahlad Street, Ansari Road
Darya Ganj, New Delhi-110002 (India)
Phone: +91-11-23279245, 43764432
Fax: +91-11-23253475
E-mail: parul.wasan@gmail.com
info@discoverypublishinggroup.com
web: www.discoverypublishinggroup.com

***First Edition:* 2011**
ISBN: 978-81-8356-799-2

Micro-Finance and Slef-Help Groups

Printed at:
Shree Balaji Art Press
Delhi

Preface

Micro-finance as a developmental and economic tool has caught the imagination of banks and other financial institutions. The social banking efforts of the Central Bank and the government particularly the expansion of self-help groups in rural areas too has gone through a phase of expansion.

The purpose of this study remains to introduce students to the exciting and challenging subject of micro-finance activities which draws on several developments of self-help groups in order to elucidate and understand the development difficulties facing the economies of the world's poor.

The book combines description and analysis for an understanding of the micro-finance issues that comprise the subject-matter of economic development.

The analysis part addresses the linkages of SHGs and Micro-finance institutions and the magnitude of the development gap between the rich and poor in the economy. The study discusses the measurement of poverty, low levels of capital accumulation, and the process of structural change in the SHGs.

We would like to thank Dr. K. Sathyalekshmi, the Principal, Sree Devi Kumari Women's College, Kuzhithurai, the management of Sree Devi Kumari Women's College, for their constant support and help.

We would also like to express our sincere thanks to Dr. S. Chellakumar Rose, Principal of Scott Christian College for his generous support that made the book possible.

We also thank Discovery Publishing House Private Ltd., New Delhi for publishing this book.

M. EDWIN GNANADHAS
M. MAHALEKSHMI

Acknowledgements

I sincerely and gratefully thank my learned guide *Dr. M. Edwin Gnanadhas.* Reader in Commerce, Scott Christian College, Nagercoil for the valuable guidance and encouragement given to me at every stage in the preparation of this work. I am sure that without his able and inspiring guidance this work couldn't have assumed its present shape.

I record my profound thanks to our former Secretary *Mr. M. Pughalzhendran,* Joint Commissioner, Incorporated and Unincorporated Devasam, Suchindram, for having accorded me permission to do this work.

I express my gratitude to our Secretary *Mr. N. Dhanabal,* Joint Commissioner, Incorporated & Unincorporated Devasam, Suchindram, for having been kind enough to encourage me to do this work with enthusiasm.

I am duty-bound to thank the Chairman, Secretary, Principal, Head of the Department and the faculty members of Department of Commerce, Scott Christian College, Nagercoil for the special interest evinced by them in providing me with all facilities to continue with my work.

I express my great debt of gratitude to our Principal *Dr. T. Chandrika Devi,* Sree Devi Kumari Womens' College, Kuzhithurai for her best wishes and encouragement to do this work.

I express my deep sense of gratitude to *Dr. X. Antony Dhanaraj,* Reader in Commerce, Scott Christian College, Nagercoil for his unfailing and timely guidance and encouragement in doing this research work.

I am immensely thankful to *Dr. M. Jesser Ebanesar,* Reader in Commerce, Scott Christian College, Nagercoil for his valuable advice and useful guidance during the course of my work.

I am grateful to *Mr. V. Sukumaran,* the former Lead Bank Manager, I.O.B., Nagercoil, *Mr. P. Chandrasekaran,* the present Lead bank Manager, I.O.B., Nagercoil, *Mr. F. Abdul Rasik*, the former DRDA Project Officer, Nagercoil,

Mr. S. Mailerum Perumal Pillai, the present DRDA Project Officer, Nagercoil, *Mr. T.K. Viswanathan*, Project Officer, Mahalir Thittam, Nagercoil, *Mr. A. Subramonia Pillai*, Assistant Project Officer, Mahalir Thittam, Nagercoil, and the Statistical Officer, Department of Statistics, the Manager, NABARD, Nagercoil for having provided me with useful information pertaining to the book.

I register my thanks to the members of the Self-help Group of Kanyakumari District for having virtually flooded me with all the relevant details regarding micro finance.

I acknowledge my deep sense of gratitude to *Prof. J. Kumarapillai*, former H.O.D of Tamil, Arignar Anna College, Aralvaymoli, Kanyakumari District, for his timely words of encouragement that enabled me to do this work with vigour.

I thank *Dr. T.M. Padmanabhan*, Department of Commerce, S.T. Hindu College, Nagercoil for the sincerity with which he looked into the subject-related aspects of the thesis.

My thanks are due to *Prof. P. Geetha*, Department of Commerce, S.T. Hindu College, Nagercoil for her words of encouragement in the preparation of the thesis.

I am beholden to *Prof. S. Nagaraja Pillai*, former H.O.D. of English, S.T. Hindu College, Nagercoil for having taken care of the linguistic elegance of the thesis.

I am highly indebted to my husband *Mr. A. Kolakalen*, and the members of my family for the great help and assistance they gave me during my research work.

I take this opportunity to thank *Prof. Mrs. C. Vijaya Prabha* Head of the Department of Commerce, SDKWC Kuzhithurai and my colleague *Prof. Mrs. S. Mariammal* SDKWC, Kuzhithurai for their words of encouragement that helped me a lot.

I am thankful to *Mrs. Jasmine Janin* for the excellent typing work done.

M. MAHALEKSHMI

Contents

CHAPTER 1 Introduction

More than one billion people around the world live in poverty. In South Asia, most of the poor are in India where the poverty rate is 52 per cent. More than 70 per cent are female. As a result women are deprived of equal access to economic opportunities. Women in the informal sector are unorganised and marginal. A new approach of helping these women micro-entrepreneurs with the support of financial institutions is becoming prominent.

India has a population of 1027.01 million with 742 million living in rural areas.[1] About 40 per cent of the rural population and 23.62 per cent of the urban population are estimated to be living below the poverty line.[2] The urban and rural poor have been dependent on money lenders for their financial needs, such as marriage in the family, illness or other emergency needs, as the formal credit system of banks, by and large, is beyond the reach of the poor. This provides an opportunity for moneylenders to exploit the situation.

The prime need of the hour is to ensure that the poor live with dignity, sufficiency and responsibility. It is also recognized that the poor people are bankable and that they themselves are likely to have a better appreciation of their socio-economic situation. The activities of Self-help Groups (SHGs) have emerged as a sustainable approach to make credit facilities available to the poor at their door step in a simple and flexible manner.

An innovative approach called "Self-help Group" with lot of promises for attacking poverty in rural areas has surfaced in the arena of development and received the attention of policy makers and the government. It is desirable in latest rural poverty alleviation programme viz., SGSY and Mahalir Thittam that formation SHG is made compulsory for availing the benefits under the programmes.

Since 1990s the new concept of group approach for development of poor people with focus on women in rural areas has come to stay and is gaining momentum as SHG approach with active support of government policy as well as apex institutions such as Reserve Bank of India (RBI), National Bank of Agriculture and Rural Development (NABARD). The experiments on SHG group approach in many Asian countries, particularly in Bangladesh have yielded a positive result with a sustainable development of poor women in particular.

An SHG is a group of about 20 people from a homogenous class, who come together for addressing their common problems. They are encouraged to make voluntary thrift on a regular basis. They use this pooled resource to make small interest bearing loans to their members. The process helps them to imbibe the essentials of financial intermediation including prioritisation of needs, setting terms and conditions and accounts keeping. This gradually builds financial discipline in all of them. They also learn to handle resources of a size that is much beyond the individual capacities of any of them.

Thus SHG members begin to appreciate that resources are limited and have a cost. The groups decide the terms of loans to their own members. Since the group's own accumulated savings are part and parcel of the aggregate loans made by the groups to their members peer pressure ensures timely repayment.

As this SHG programme receives more significance towards development of poor in general and women in particular and show positive impact on their economic development it will be used to assess the impact of poverty alleviation programmes on the development of rural poor in Kanyakumari district of Tamil Nadu.

SELF-HELP GROUPS: EVOLUTION, CONCEPT AND FEATURES

Evolution of SHGs

The genesis of SHGs could be traced to "Mutual Aid" in Indian village community. In traditional rural societies, self-help takes various forms. Activities like housing/farm operations, which have to be completed within a stipulated time, depend upon such arrangements. Likewise, people share implements required in agricultural production. Sharing of irrigation water/bullocks necessitates a management based on Self-Help. However, in the West, the theoretical approach to collective action was among others, developed by Olson and he says people will participate in collective action when they are organized in small groups when the expected private benefits from the collective action exceed the expected private costs of participation.[3]

The existence of traditional saving groups has been well documented and has a long and successful history in India. Informal SHGs oriented to saving and credit functions are not a new phenomenon.[4] Some forms of credit instruments were in operation even before 1904 when the Co-operative Credit Societies Act was passed. Credit instruments such as Nidhis and Chit Funds were popular, especially in South India. They had several distinguishing features, such as, encouraging thrift, mobilizing small savings and inculcating in the members the habits of punctuality and planning for future. The useful role played by these instruments in the rural areas as important sources of credit to people with moderate needs has been well recognized.

The SHG is defined as a voluntary group valuing personal interactions and mutual aid as a means of altering or ameliorating the problems perceived as alterable, pressing and personal by most of its participants.[5] These groups are voluntary associations of people formed to attain certain collective goals that could be economic, social or both. The policy planners and development planners cherish the myth that poor people do not have the spirit of thrift; but recent reports from different parts of the globe challenge this.[6]

Since the SHGs in India are informal groups, their legal status has not been defined. What they initially intended was to bring together people, particularly economically weaker sections and to undertake activities of mutual interest. Members of SHGs have no risk taking ability, hardly anything to offer as guarantee against availing loans from formal Rural Financial Institutions (RFIs) and limited earning opportunities. However, thrift, credit and income generating activities emerged as the major activities of the SHGs. In other words, the SHGs evolved a system for collective savings, group consumption credit, as well as, integrating social and economic goals among small groups.

The initial growth of SHGs has been in areas where they received support from Non-Governmental Organisations (NGOs). The NGO supported not only in the formation of SHGs but also in identifying economic activities, imparting training, and even financial support in the initial stage. The critical areas in forming the groups at the beginning were their size and composition, homogeneity, group discipline, saving habits and sustainability. By offering savings services, a financial institution can promote greater customer loyalty and loan repayment discipline, thus reducing the institution's cost of funds for on-lending and overall transaction cost. Moreover, RFIs can also improve their viability by expanding their volume of business.[7] Subsequently, the SHGs have been linked with banks for saving and credit operations. Bank linkage model evolved as a core strategy that could be used by the banking system for increasing its outreach to the poorest of the poor who were hitherto getting by-passed by it.[8]

Concept of SHG

SHG is a small voluntary association of rural people, preferably women folk from the same socio-economic background. They come together for the purpose of solving their common problems through self-help and mutual help in the SHGs. Usually the maximum number of members in one SHG is 20. They undertake economic activities such as thrift and credit and use of common asset on a basis of equality nurturing trust.

The Self-help Groups are voluntary associations of people formed to attain a collective goal. People who are homogenous with respect to social background, heritage, caste or traditional occupation come together for a common cause to raise and manage resources for the benefit of the group members.

The process by which the group of people with a common objective are facilitated to come together in order to participate in the development activities, i.e. savings, credit, income generation, etc., is called Group Formation.

Although the SHGs can be formed for any development activity, for the financial institutions to use them as a conduit for banking activities, the SHGs should be practicing thrift and credit and be familiar with money management.[9]

Features of SHGs

Generally, SHGs encompass several activities of men and women but the Indian focus is on financial aspects of SHGs. In addition to India, this financial SHG concept is being promoted in Bangladesh, Indonesia, Thailand, Philippines, Nepal, Sri Lanka, etc. The Salient features of SHGs are:

1. Homogenous in terms of economic status and interest and an affinity group.
2. Small in size and their membership per group range from 10 to 20 people.
3. They are non-political and voluntary and follow democratic culture.

4. They hold weekly meetings and mostly during non-working hours.
5. They have transparency among themselves and they have the collective accountability of financial transactions in the group.
6. Functions
   (*a*) Conduct regular weekly meetings;
   (*b*) Promote saving attitude and habit among the members;
   (*c*) Indulge in credit management;
7. Build the common fund slowly and systematically; and
8. Establish linkage with bank and government departments.

A typical SHG model is depicted in Fig. 1.1. Some of the features might vary from one SHG to another promoted by various NGOs, banks, etc.

Significance of SHGs

The SHGs are necessary to overcome exploitation, create confidence for economic self-reliance in the poor, particularly in women who are mostly invisible in the social structure. The SHGs become the basis of action and change and build a relationship of mutual trust between the promoting organization and the rural poor through constant contact and genuine efforts.[10] Credit delivery through thrift and credit groups (SHGs) emerges as an alternative to the existing system of credit disbursement by the banks. SHGs have been found to help and inculcate among their members sound habits of thrift, saving and banking.[11]

Self-help approach is a fast gaining acceptance internationally as the most appropriate instrument to reach out to the poorest of the poor in a most effective way.[12] Experience in various countries has brought to light the fact that SHGs play a significant role in mobilizing substantial

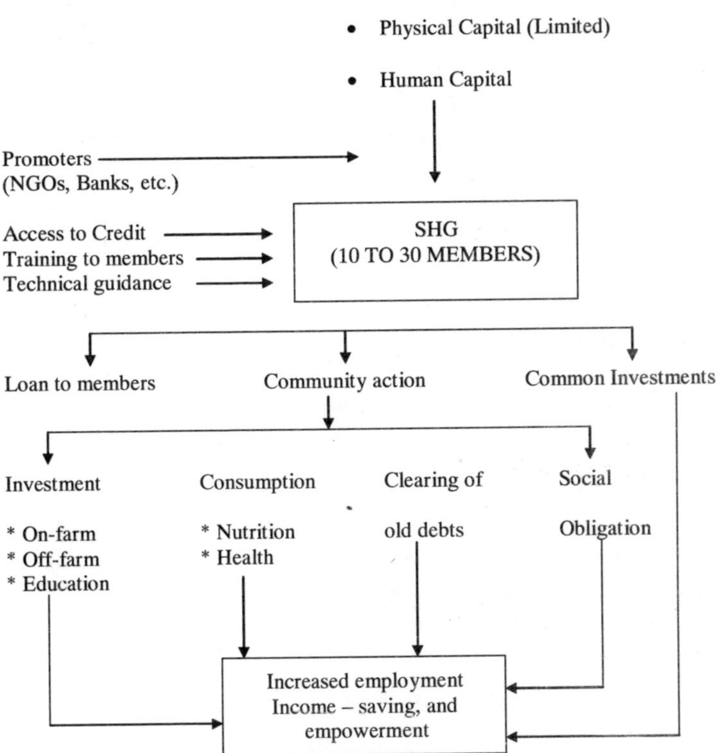

Fig. 1.1. A Typical SHG Model

amounts of saving and providing loans to the members. SHGs have also been able to bring about positive improvement in a number of social indicators such as literacy and health.[13]

The SHGs promote participatory credit management and fill a vacuum created by the ineffective, rigid formal credit necessity of adopting a flexible mechanism sensitive to the needs and conditions of the people for whom these are meant. Rescheduling of loans in times of genuine hardships, reorganizing the consumption requirements of the people along with their production needs and the need to address social problems are all considered.[14]

The benefits of SHGs, that have primarily been formed in India as micro-credit groups for economic empowerment of women and the weaker sections are: that poor; have access to large quantum of resources; provide a window for better technology and skill upgradation, have access to various promotional assistance and assurance of freedom, self-reliance and empowerment. Collectivisation implies cohesion of the group and enables the members of the group to perceive common interests and act collectively. In contrast to formal organizations, self-help is highly personal, non-hierarchical and without division of labour. Self-help favours experience over expertise.[15]

MICRO-FINANCE

Micro-finance refers to the entire range of financial and non-financial services including skill upgradation and entrepreneurship development, rendered to rural poor for enabling them to overcome poverty. The Indian micro-finance is dominated by SHGs and their linkage to banks. The NGOs play a vital role in making linkages between SHGs and banks.

The structure of rural financial market in India is dualistic consisting of both formal and informal financial intermediaries. A consensus is growing among researches that the formal financial sector is not effectively serving the rural population in the Third World countries.[16] This is mainly attributed to the failure of financial intermediaries fulfilling their basic functions namely, production credit to finance income generating activities, consumption credit to maintain and expand human productive capacity and quality saving schemes for increasing risk bearing capacity of the rural households. Moreover, these institutions have failed to promote any of their social objectives.[17] To reach the poor, institutional innovations are needed that enables services to be expanded, while substantially reducing transaction costs for both financial institutions and clients.[18] In many countries in the world, micro-credit programmes have succeeded in generating self-employment by providing access to small capital to people living in poverty.[19]

The performance of formal financial institutions particularly in their lending to the poor in India has been unsatisfactory. They face a number of constraints in broadening their services to the poor. As a result of the inaccessibility of the formal banking system to the poor, micro-financial institutions emerged, which act as an impetus for community action.[20] There has been a surge of interest in micro-finance in the recent past particularly in the context of reaching the poor families in a more effective way.[21] As an informal supplementary credit delivery mechanism by lending at a group level, the Self-help Groups came into existence.

Finance is basic to any economic activity. The basic philosophy of rural finance is the dispensation of loans at a concessional rate through administrative control targeting the rural people engaged either in agricultural or non-agricultural activities. But, it is felt that a large number of poverty stricken people and particularly women, who constitute a significant number, still remain outside the ambit of institutional finance. In order to give a new approach to rural finance, NABARD had introduced the Self-help Groups in 1992, which is generally treated as finance to a small group. This new approach, in other words, is known as micro-credit.

Micro-credit programmes extend small loans to poor people for self-employment projects that generate income, allowing them to care for themselves and their families. In most cases, micro-credit programmes offer a combination of services and resources to their clients in addition to credit for self-employment. These often include savings, training networking and peer support. It is ironical that micro-enterprises are often unorganised, decentralized and unprotected and their contribution to the economy often remains unorganised.

In February 1997, a summit was convened in Washington to review and give direction for financing to the poorest people in the under-developed countries. The summit defined its goal to Micro-finance those "programmes that provide credit for self-employment and other financial and business services (including savings and other technical assistance) to very poor persons. Micro-level financial schemes help people themselves by starting small income generation projects and activities.[22]

The maximum experimentation with micro-credit can be seen in Bangladesh, where it has been extensively used for reaching the poorest sections of the society. It has proved to be a most powerful weapon to fight poverty. During the seventies many initiatives were taken in developed and developing countries in Asia, Africa and Latin America. The approach of micro-credit consisted of Self-help groups, Revolving Savings and Credit Associations (ROSCAS), Solidarity Groups, Money Store, etc. Some of the examples outside India are Philippine Commercial and Industrial Bank, Rural Bank of Ghana and Grameen Bank (Bangladesh).[23] The Grameen Bank set up in 1976 by Muhammad Yunus, is one of the most popular models for providing micro-credit to poor. At present 90 per cent of the members are women.[24]

In India, Self-employment Women's Association (SEWA) in Gujarat and Madhya Pradesh, Mysore Resettlement Development Agency (MYRADA) in Karnataka, Professional Assistance for Development Action (PRADAN) in Rajasthan, Association of Sarva Seva Farms (ASSEFA) in Tamil Nadu, New Public School Society in Uttar Pradesh, and other organisations took up the initiative. The credit needs of groups are met in a convenient, flexible and cost-effective way.

The NABARD's efforts of improving the access of the rural poor for formal banking services through SHGs has gathered momentum during the last few years. It not only extends

100 per cent refinance facilities to the banks at concessional interest rate, but it has also taken various promotional initiatives to expand SHG-Bank linkage programme.[25] Small Industries Development Bank of India (SIDBI) also extends credit facilities through NGOs and more than 150 NGOs have availed credit facilities from SIDBI for on-lending to small borrowers.[26]

The Department of Women and Child Development launched the Indira Mahila Yojana (IMY) in 1995 as a central sector project for the holistic empowerment of women in 200 blocks. Under this programme, efforts are being made for setting up of SHGs of women. The IMY aims to fill up the gaps where suitable NGOs are not available to take up micro-credit programmes.[27] Rashtriya Mahila Kosh (RMK) was set up in March (1993), with the objectives of extending credit limits to poor women through NGOs Women Development Corporations (WDC), Co-operative Societies and Indira Mahila Block Samitees and taking up other promotional and advocacy roles to achieve economic self reliance for women. Credit facilities are extended at eight per cent interest, which in turn, is lent to SHGs at the interest rate of 12 per cent per annum. The SHGs can lend to the women members at an interest rate not exceeding the State Bank of India (SBI) interest rate on unsecured advances. The NGOs can also extend loan facilities to individual women where SHGs do not exist.[28]

EMPOWERMENT OF WOMEN

The Global Conference on Women's Empowerment, 1988, highlighted empowerment as the surest way of making women "partners in development". Development on the other hand should ultimately become a process of empowerment. Empowerment is an active process enabling women to realise their full identify and power in all spheres of life.

Although women form nearly half of the human capital in the country, they are still the most deprived and neglected segments of society despite the constitutional guarantee for equal rights and privileges for men and women. Women continue to be victims of a process of economic, social, cultural and political marginalisation. Women are viewed as home-makers and are not encouraged to undertake professions to which men have natural access. On the other hand, half of the world's food is produced by women working in the fields and they constitute 1/3 of the world's labour force. Although a woman does double the amount of work and contributes doubly to the economy, she is considered a burden and instances of female infanticide and foeticide bear testimony to this. Empowerment is a multifaceted process encompassing aspects such as enhancing awareness, increasing access to resources – economic, social and political. It comprises an equally important component of mobilisation and organization of women into groups, because these groups form the basis for solidarity, strength and collective action.

Empowerment of women is a critical factor in the eradication of poverty, as the women are the key contributors to the economy and to combating poverty through both remunerative and unremunerative work at home, in the community and in the work place.[29] Gainful employment has been viewed as a critical entry point for women's integration in development.[30]

Women's participation in income generating activities is believed to increase their status and decision-making power. With employment women do not remain as 'objects' of social change but become 'agents' of it. They cease from being 'consumers' of economic goods and services and turn into 'producers'. They participate in social reproduction as well as in reproduction of labour for the next generation.[31]

In many cases, micro-credit has been a crucial element in increasing women's economic opportunities. When done well, it gives women the ability to make a living on a sustainable basis. Micro-credit could unleash the economic potential of hundreds of millions of the world's poorest.

The country's response to the challenges of equality, development and peace is the "empowerment strategy". The challenge before the society is to evolve strategies to break the stereotypes of the past by solving problems of poverty, illiteracy, environmental degradation, violence, gender inequality, etc. Hence, Self-help Groups and micro-credit should be seen as components of a solution to accelerate the socio-economic development particularly, of the rural poor women in India. A judicious mix of micro-credit along with other activities with emphasis on development and empowerment strategies and processes would certainly make micro-credit an effective instrument of social and economic development particularly of women in a holistic and integrated manner.[32]

In the light of this, a world-wide effort to reach many of the poorest families with micro-level was launched. Eighteen months after the Beijing Conference on 2-4, February 1997, more than 2900 people representing 1500 institutions from 137 countries gathered at the Micro-credit Summit in Washington, DC. Together they set the ambitious goal of reaching 100 million of the world's poorest families, especially the women of those families with credit of self-employment and other financial and business services by the year 2005.

STATEMENT OF THE PROBLEM

Integrated Rural Development Programme (IRDP) launched for poverty alleviation in India was a target-oriented programme with the focus on identifying the poorest of the poor and helping them to acquire productive assets through bank loans and subsidy from the government. The underlying assumption was that lack of productive assets as responsible for the poor being unable to better their lot. The IRDP, however, was not as successful as was visualized.

In 1982-83, Development of Women and Children in Rural Area (DWCRA) was launched in 50 districts as a sub-scheme of IRDP. This was an attempt to involve women more intensively in economic activities. The focus of DWCRA was on economic activities for rural women to be taken up as they had never before undertaken like going to the bank, buying an asset, keeping accounts, etc. Another object of the group was to enable women to take a larger amount of loan, so that, by pooling their individual loans, they could start a viable non-farm activity. The DWCRA scheme was implemented, like IRDP, through bank branches and District Rural Development Agencies (DRDA).

The DWCRA too met with a limited success. The scheme as a whole failed to take off. It was seen that the economic activities, although well thought out, were not really feasible in the long run. It was observed that women were not ready to take on entrepreneurial roles; all they wanted was small loans for specific requirements, which were mainly for consumption purposes.

Despite these schemes and several others [Training of Rural Youth for Self-Employment (TRYSEM), Supply of Improved Toolkits to Rural Artisans (SITRA)], the credit and poverty problem in the rural area continues. According to the Government of India's Ministry of Rural Development,

> "While the antipoverty programmes have been strengthened in successive years and while in terms of percentage, poverty levels have reduced from 56.44 per cent of India's population in 1973-74 to 37.27 per cent in 1993-94, the number of rural poor has, more or less, remained static and is estimated to be about 244 million people. The rural poor are still dependent on informal sources of credit despite an impressive expansion of bank branch network. Although this dependence has come down from 83.7 per cent of the rural population in 1961 to 36 per cent in 1991, the problem still persists. It is not difficult to reckon the effect of such a large percentage of poor on the country's development. Obviously, the situation needs to be redressed quickly. It is in this context that the self-employment programmes assume significance for, they alone can provide income to the rural poor on a sustainable basis."

The major problem with most schemes for poverty alleviation and channelling credit to the rural areas seems to be that they are not based on realistic assumptions and analysis of the rural credit markets. In earlier schemes, like IRDP, DWCRA, etc., the beneficiaries perceived the loan as a grant. They did not feel the responsibility of time or the mechanism for monitoring the repayment. This led to poor loan recovery and resulted in the scheme becoming non-viable.[34] In contrast, the repayment of loans in micro-credit schemes using SHGs is reported to be satisfactory from almost all places. This may be due to the fact that the concept of SHG in Micro-Credit Schemes is based on the theory of asymmetric information and peer monitoring.

The credit needs of the rural poor are determined in a complex socio-economic milieu where it is difficult to adopt project lending approach and where the dividing line between credit for consumption and production purposes is blurred. Under the circumstances, a non-formal agency in the form of self-help groups of the poor could emerge as a promising partner of the formal agencies.

Dissatisfaction with the result of many formal credit programmes has stimulated searches for modalities that may provide effective financial services to rural poor particularly to women. Taking the lesson from the experiences of other developing countries like Bangladesh, Indonesia, Bolivia and Philippines where combination of formal and informal finance provides sustained and valuable services to poor, a few NGOs in India, started experimenting the innovative scheme of Self-help Groups which are also called as Thrift and Credit Groups.

In India, over the years, various poverty alleviation programmes have been initiated by government as well as voluntary organizations. Despite these efforts, not much difference is seen in the magnitude of poverty. Micro-credit has now emerged as a financial strategy to reach the urban and rural poor and is emerging as a movement at the global level. Over the past two decades, micro-credit has acquired greater dimension and recognition as an instrument for meeting the credit needs of the poor for starting up their Income Generating Activities (IGA) or Micro-Enterprises (ME). The institution of Self-Help Groups (SHGs) has provided strength to Micro-Credit System.[35]

Presiding over the Micro-Credit Summit, 2001, organized by All-India Women's Conference, New Delhi, Shri Yeshwant Sinha, the them Minister of Finance, Government of India, stressed the need for micro-credit programmes as a tool for poverty alleviation and empowerment of women.

Micro-enterprises are important sources of income and employment for a significant proportion of the rural poor. In fact, this sub-sector is perceived to be an essential part of survival strategy of poor households. The relationship between micro-enterprises and poverty reduction is coming up for serious consideration among the policy makers and development programme implementing.

Families below poverty line, the landless and the poorest of the poor do not have access to formal credit institutions. The informal credit institutions include money lenders, landlords, traders and middlemen. The formal sector includes commercial banks, cooperative banks, cooperative thrift and credit societies, regional rural banks and Government agencies. Nationalisation of banks in 1969 changed the pattern of credit delivery with high priority given to income generation for the poor. However, the banks have failed to reach them. The situation of poor women is worse. Their lack of credit worthiness is a factor that leads to their exclusion. Such poor household and especially women need to be brought into the mainstream of the credit system, to avoid economic exploitation by the informal credit institutions.

A credit is definitely an entry point for upliftment programmes for the rural poor. As SHGs have regular transactions with banks, it is easy to extend credit to them through subsidy linked target-oriented schemes such as Swarnajayanthi Gram Swarozgar Yojana (SGSY) and

Mahalir Thittam. Indeed, many micro-finance programmes observe the motto "Savings First, Credit Later".

This is the approach underlying NABARD's "Linking banks with Self-help Groups" programmes, which requires the group members to save regularly, pool these savings and lend them to one another, thereby acquiring credit discipline and experience, before depositing the savings in banks as part collateral for obtaining bulk loans from the banks. It is cheaper for the banks to leave the retailing to the group, which is also responsible for collection and repayment.

Despite the vast expansion of the formal credit system in India, the dependence of the rural poor on money lenders continues is some areas, particularly for meeting urgent credit needs mainly for consumption purposes. For various reasons, the credit flow to these sections of the population for meeting their credit requirements has not been institutionalised. The credit needs of the rural poor are determined in a complex socio-economic milieu, wherein it is difficult to adopt project lending approach as followed by banks and wherein the dividing line between credit for consumption and production purposes is blurred. In the circumstances, a non-formal agency of credit supply to the poor in the form of "Self-help Groups" of the poor could emerge as promising partner of the formal agencies. The present study attempts to analyse the impact of micro-finance on women Self-help Groups in Kanyakumari district of Tamil Nadu.

In this context, a research study was taken up to document the experiences of the SHGs in promoting micro-enterprises through micro-credit interventions and evaluate the impact of the programme.

SCOPE OF THE STUDY

The current study, which is basically a research study, provided an opportunity to bring an awareness among women about their situation, discrimination of rights and opportunities as a step towards gender equality. Collective awareness-building provides a sense of group identity and the power of working as a group. Collectivisation implies cohesion of the group. Cohesion enables the members of the group to perceive common interests and act collectively. It facilitates :

- Capacity building and skill development especially the ability to plan, make decisions, organize, manage and carry out activities, deal with people and institutions in the world around them.
- Participation and greater control and decision making power in the home, community and society.
- Wider scope for the NGOs to attempt group approach.
- Creation of favourable policy environment for SHGs to easily open their bank account.
- Constitution of high powered task force to make recommendations with regard to policy and regulation of the micro-finance sector.

This research study help women to strengthen their economic activities, create positive linkages and support for access to raw materials, skill training, marketing opportunities and credit needs.

The findings and suggestions will throw light on certain broad features of the country and as such the study may be of practical use in formulating better plans.

OBJECTIVES OF THE STUDY

The main objective of the study is to analyse the impact of micro-finance on women SHGs Tamil Nadu. The specific objectives of the study are:

(*i*) To study the role of Micro-Finance assistance to SHGs in Kanyakumari District;

(*ii*) To analyse the performances of rural development programmes like SGSY and Mahalir Thittam through SHGs in the study district;

(*iii*) To find out the impact of the micro-finance on the women Self-Help Groups in the same district;

(*iv*) To review the problems in the implementation of micro-finance activities in Tamil Nadu; and

(*v*) To suggest effective measures for the successful implementation of micro-finance activities through SHGs in Tamil Nadu.

METHODOLOGY

Construction of Interview Schedule

The study involves the collection of data from both the primary and secondary sources. The primary data were collected from the beneficiaries of SGSY schemes in Kanyakumari district of Tamil Nadu. For this purpose a comprehensive interview schedule was prepared – an interview schedule of the members of the SHGs. This interview schedule was designed to elicit information regarding thrift and credit activities of members, group leaders' activities, micro-enterprises initiated by the members. The interview schedule was pre-tested with SHG members and reframed in the light of the experience and insights gained after conducting the pre-testing.

The data pertaining to incremental income, assets created and employment generated were elicited through the interview schedule administered on the micro-entrepreneurs both during the pre credit and post credit period.

Collection of Secondary Data

The secondary data were collected from reports, records, books and journals relating to the performances of the SGSY scheme for a period of six years (1999-2000 to 2000-2005 i.e., from the inception of the scheme to the present.

SHG Model

There are three models of Self-help Groups. They are Direct linkage with banks, NGO as facilitator and NGO as intermediary. In Kanyakumari district three blocks were selected. From the selected blocks 15 SHGs consisting of the three different models and each model represented by five groups were analysed.

Sampling Design

The authors have adopted multi-stage random sampling method to select the respondent self-help group members.

A total of 45 SHGs consisting of 15 Direct linkage SHGs, 15 NGO facilitator SHGs and 15 NGO as intermediary SHGs were selected in 3 selected blocks of Kanyakumari district. Five individual Swarnogzories were identified in each group for interview purpose. A total of 225 individual beneficiaries of SGSY scheme were interviewed with the pre-tested questionnaire. A discussion was held with selected officials of the Blocks, Bank, Lead Bank, DRDA, NGO's NABARD, Block Development Office etc. The collected data were analysed with the suitable statistical tools.

Tools of Analysis

For interpreting, summarising and analysing the collected data, the tools such as paired 't' test correlation analysis, regression analysis, chi-square test and ratio analysis were extensively used. Besides, percentage, mean standard deviation, co-efficient of variation, graphs and diagrams were used wherever necessary to compare the data. Analysis was also carried out to compare the findings of the urban and rural areas and the performance of micro-enterprises among different categories of activity studied under different sectors.

SWOT analysis was done to assess the strengths and weaknesses of the SHGs in Micro-Credit Management.

LIMITATIONS

The data for the present study were collected through personal interview method. Since the beneficiary groups did not maintain proper accounts and most of them were uneducated, the possibility of data bias exists and hence the data collected would only be an approximation of actual facts.

Due to time constraint, only 30 groups could be formed for the study. Their performance and functioning might not be uniform as compared to the existing groups functioning in the Kanyakumari district.

CHAPTERISATION

Chapter One consists of introduction, concept and evolution of SHGs, emergence of micro-credit, women empowerment, statement of the problem, objectives of the study, design of the study, the scope and the limitations of the study.

Chapter Two gives the review of the past studies relating to the SHGs and Micro-credit and SGSY.

The profile of the Kanyakumari district is presented in Chapter Three.

Chapter Four evaluates the performance of the SHGs under SGSY in Kanyakumari district.

Chapter Five analyses the impact of micro-finance of SGSY on SHG members.

Chapter Six presents the summary of the findings, bringing out the suggestions and policy implications.

REFERENCES

1. Census of India, July, 2001, www.census.india.com.
2. Mishra and Purrie, 55th NSS Round, 2001.
3. Olson, Manuor, *The Logic of Collective Action: Public Goods and the Theory of Groups,* New York, Schaken Books, 1971, p.15.
4. Desai, Bhupat, M., and N.V. Namboodiri, *Organising and Management of Rural Financial Sector: Text, Cases and Exercises,* New Delhi, Oxford and IBH Publishing Company Pvt., Ltd., 2001, p. 52.
5. Smith, D.H., and K. Pillheimer, "Self-Help Groups as Social Movement Organisations: Social Structure and Social Change", *Research in Social Movements, Conflicts and Change,* Vol. 5, No. 2, 1983, p. 35.

6. Kaladha, K., "Micro-Finance in India: Design, Structure and Governance", *Economic and Political Weekly,* Vol. 32, No. 42, October 18, 1997, p. 21.
7. Desai, B.M., and J.W. Mellor, "Institutional Finance for Agriculture Development: An Analytical Survey of Critical Issues", *Food Policy Review 1,* U.S.A.: Washington D.C., International Food Policy Research Institute, 1993, p. 18.
8. Nanda, Y.C., *Role of Banks in Rural Development in the New Millennium,* Mumbai: National Bank for Agriculture and Rural Development, 2000, p. 12.
9. Srinivasan, Girija, *Training Programme on Credit and Micro-Enterprises Development for the NGOs and Officials of IMY,* Lucknow: Bankers Institute for Rural Development (BIRD), 1997, pp. 18-19.
10. Gupta, R.C., *Guidelines for Field Workers on Management of Self-Help Savings and Credit Groups,* New Delhi L. Friedrich Ebert Stiffung, 1993, p. 3.
11. Rashtriya Mahila Kosh, *Annual Report,* New Delhi: Veerendra Printers, 1995, p.11.
12. Satish, P., and P. Das, "Linkage of SHGs with Formal Financial Agencies Experience of Other Countries in Asia", Working Paper 4, Lucknow, Bankers Institute of Rural Development, 1997, p. 2.
13. Shivakumar, L., "Self-Help Groups", *Social Welfare,* Vol.XI, No. 6, October 6, 1995, pp. 8-10.
14. Dwaraki and Kumarasan, B., "Self-Help Groups – Quo Vadis?", *Social Welfare,* Vol. 44, No. 3, June 1997, p. 40.
15. Murugan, K.R., and Dharmalingam, "Self-Help Groups – New Women's Movement in Tamil Nadu", *Social Welfare,* Vol. 47, No. 45, 2000, pp. 9-12.
16. Bouman, F.J.A., "Informal Savings and Credit Arrangements in Developing Countries: Observations from Sri Lanka". In Dale W. Adams, G.H. Garham and J.D. Von Pischke (eds.), *Undermining Rural Development with Cheap Credit,* London, Westview Press, 1984, pp. 40-42.
17. Desai, Bhupat, M., and N.V. Namboodiri, "Whither Rural Financial Institutions", *Economic and Political Weekly,* Vol. 31, No. 31, August 3, 1996, p. 10.
18. Zeller, Manfred and Manohar Sharma, *Rural Finance and Poverty Alleviation, Food Policy Report,* USA: Washington, D.C., International Food Policy Research Institute, 1998, p. 6.
19. 52/194 passed in December 1997, 1998", in Count down 2005, *Newsletter of the Micro-Credit-Summit Campaign,* Vol.1 No.3, February-March, 1998, p. 21.

20. Swarup, V., "Micro-Finance could Become a Macro Mess", *The Economic Times,* Ahmedabad, February 26, 2001, p. 7.
21. Kaladhar, K., "Micro-Finance in India: Design, Structure and Government", *Economic and Political Weekly,* Vol. 32, No. 42, October 19, 1997, p. 5.
22. World Bank, "Introducing Savings in Micro-Credit Institutions: When and How?", CGAP Focus Note, U.S.A.: Washington, D.C., Consultative Group to Assist the Poorest of the Poor, 1997, p. 25.
23. Edwards, John, H.Y., *Rotating Credit / Associations and Lotteries as Financial Instruments for the Poor,* Tulane University, Economics Department, new Orleans, La processed, 1989.
24. Hossain, Mahabub, Credit for Alleviation of Rural Poverty: The Grameen Bank in Bangladesh, *Research Report No. 65,* Washington, D.C. : International Food Policy Research Institute, Processed, 1998.
25. National Bank for Agriculture and Rural Development (NABARD), Mumbai: *Report of the Task Force on Supportive Policy and Regulatory Framework for Micro-Finance,* 1999.
26. Small Industries Development Bank of India (SIDBI) *Annual Report,* New Delh, 1998.
27. Department of Women and Child Development, *Annual Report Part-IV,* Ministry of Human Resource Development, Government of India, 1996, pp.49-51 and 93.
28. *Hindustan Times*, July 13, 2001, p. 9.
29. United Nations, Fourth World Conference on Women, The Beijings Declaration and the Platform for Action, Chennai, Department of Public Information, New York, 1996, pp. 25-39.
30. Devadas, R.P., *Management of Development Programmes for Women and Children through Home Science,* Vol. 5, Coimbatore: Sri Avinashilingam Trust Institutions, 1986, pp. 225-227.
31. International Labour Organisation (ILO), "Women's Participation in Economic Activity", Geneva: *World Employment Programme Research Working Paper No. 42,* 1984, p. 17.
32. Sinha, Archana, "Types of SHGs and Their Work", Social Welfare, February, 2002, p. 16.
33. Government of India, Swarnajayanti Gram Swarozar Yojana, *Guidelines*, New Delhi, Ministry of Rural Development, 1999, p. 10.
34. Rath, N., "Garibiaa Hatao: Can IRDP Do It?", *Economic and Political Weekly,* Vol. No.6, February 9, 1985, pp. 238-246.
35. Joshi, S.C., "Micro-Credit Not Charity", *Social Welfare*, February, 2002, pp. 12-14.

Review of Literature

INTRODUCTION

Providing women with financial credit and helping them to set up small enterprises thus enabling them to increase their earning is considered a means of poverty reduction and economic empowerment. Many NGOs have initiated the empowerment process of poor women by organizing them into groups and building their capacity to improve their lives through micro-credit programmes. Evaluation is undertaken to know how the programme is being implemented and what can be done to remove the constraints, if any. Evaluation is thus a kind of achievement audit and mostly takes place after the programme has run for a specific period.

It is desirable to review the relevant literature while handling a research problem. A review of literature places a research study in its proper perspective by showing the amount of work already carried out in the related areas of the study.

REVIEW OF LITERATURE

The following are the studies which enabled the researcher to undertake this study:

Schenk, Loes and Sandbergen (1991) observe that, the concept of women's interests assumes compatibility of interest based on biological similarities. In fact the position of women in society depends on a variety of different criteria, such as class and ethnicity as well as gender, and consequently the interest they may have in common may be determined as much by their class position or their ethnic identity as by their biological similarity as women.[1]

Hamsa, N. (1992) observes that, the concern for women in economic and social development arises from the relative exclusion of women from the development process in different countries across the world. According to all indicators, social, economic, and legal status of women as a group has been lagging behind their male counterparts. Therefore, the task of integrating women in development requires simultaneous efforts to improve their condition from both economic and social angles. This is so because women's multiple roles put them in a position to be influenced by and to influence social and economic processes. Broadly, women's participation in development calls for arrangements that would lighten women's domestic work load in order to release them for other economic and socially productive work. Clearly, the task of addressing the foregoing twin problems require measures that would not only create more opportunities for women for income generation, but also for protective measures for those in the work field. This calls for special provisions for women in self-employment and for education and training policies to that effect together improvements in wages and working conditions. One of the approaches for the integration of women in economic and social development, therefore, is to identify opportunities that would provide women with more avenues for self-employment and a conscious effort towards the development of entrepreneurship among women.[2]

Sinha, S.L.N. (1993) observes that though women have contributed significantly in every sphere of life, yet for various historical, social, religious and cultural reasons and inspite of many constitutional guarantees and legislative measures, women still remain backward and shorn of their rightful place in society. The finding of the National Status for Women Committee (1975) has revealed that the status of women has been declining steadily. This observation indicates that the initial recognition of women's rights, which emerged during the freedom struggle and was expressed in the constitution, has run into sands. Indian society's inherent male chauvinism is among the distressing facts of life that have not changed and has become all the more pernicious having crept into the process of planned development. The extreme reticence of our women – a euphemism for the voicelessness into which they are thrust – is a throw off of the kind of feminine culture we foster to crop up again and again in various circumstances, affecting the course of justice.[3]

Jain, R.K. (1994) is of the opinion that women have at last been recognized as a target group for the promotion of economic self reliance. For assuring equality, dignity, justice, prosperity and stability, the contribution of women has to be viewed in a wider perspective. Various studies have indicated that money is actually safe in the hands of women. Studies have also shown that contribution to the household normally increases with an increase in women's income. It has rightly been said that the slogan for economic upliftment of women has to be 'Doing things with them' and not 'Doing things for them'.[4]

Mohanty, Manoranjan (1995) observes that, the concept of empowerment implies formal rather than substantive power and it involves an external upper level agency to grant power rather than people below seizing it in the course of struggle. Above all this concept is part of the political philosophy of the new economic globalization of western capitalism. The term 'empowerment', i.e., giving power to a certain unprivileged section of society came to be used.[5]

As stated by Gulati, Urvashi (1995), Describing the Constitution (73rd and 74th Amendment) Acts as the most revolutionary step towards the empowerment of women, particularly rural women, has secured the participation of one million women in decision-making at the grassroots level.

Any poverty reduction and growth policy which fails to address itself to women is bound to be less effective. It cannot afford to ignore women. Calling for a radical transformation through awareness on gender issues for a gender-just society, she feels women's own perceptions of themselves also need to be changed.[6]

Pinto, Marina (1995) observes that implicit in participation is empowerment or transfer of power to the people. Empowering is development of skills and abilities of people to enable them to manage better, have a say in or negotiates with existing development delivery systems. The empowerment process encompasses several mutually reinforcing components but begins with and is supported by economic independence which implies access to and control over production resources. Second component of empowerment is knowledge and awareness, the third is self-image and the final is autonomy. In India, the plight of women is no better than that of women in other developing countries. In a patriarchal society such as ours, there exists the unfounded belief that man is the bread-winner of the family. This unfortunate state of affairs stems from the fact that the role of women in overall development has not been fully understood nor has it been given weightage in the struggle to fight poverty, inequality and injustice. The World Bank Report (August 1989) clearly underlines the fact that 'women already contribute far more economically than is usually recognised' and that their capacity to work is particularly constrained and their productivity reduced by culture and tradition and even at times by law or policy. This is as true of Indian women as those elsewhere.[7]

Puhazhendi, V. (1995) studies 10 SHGs and five bank branches in Karnataka and Tamil Nadu and concludes that the intermediation of SHGs reduced the time spent by bank personnel in identification of borrowers, documentation, follow up and recoveries effecting 40 per cent reduction in the transaction cost of the bank, as compared to direct lending to individual borrowers. Transaction cost of borrowers was reduced by 85 per cent.[8]

Indian Bank (1995) had conducted a similar study in Tamil Nadu, covering 45 branches of their bank and 101 SHGs. The study examined only the transaction costs of the branches under different models for credit delivered for medium term loans up to Rs. 25,000. It concluded that lending to SHGs, which lend to borrowers with NGO acting as non financial intermediary, resulted in saving of transaction costs to the extent of 45 per cent as compared to lending under government sponsored programmes and other direct lending projects.[9]

The Bank performance improvement study under the Maharashtra Rural Credit Project (MRCP) concluded that with SHG intermediation, the transaction and risk costs of the advances of the rural branches could be brought down that could help turn around many loss making rural branches (BIRD, 1996)[10]

Sinha, S.L.N. (1997) says that, in the past fifty years after India's independence, development planning for women has straddled theories as disparate as welfare, development, equity, efficiency and empowerment. The institutional structures have undergone changes in response to the evolving concepts. These have changed from welfare to empowerment and beyond. The State first reviewed women as a 'handicapped' category and as appropriate recipients of welfare doles. Today, the State has accepted women's empowerment, women as active agents participating in and guiding their own development. In fact, women's demand for greater respect and enhanced rights is a part of a wider democratic movement. Our social organisations involved in the task of women's emancipation and, uplift should lay great stress on creating consciousness among the people to treat women at par in all walks of life. The Government should be a helping hand to their efforts, particularly in field of constant monitoring and evaluation of progress in the direction of raising the social status of women. Cruelties against them, including dowry deaths, should become things of the past in the new milieu of our social life.[11]

Agarwal, Bina (1998) says that the term "Empowerment' has been used variously and often loosely in academic writing and by social action groups across the world. In the present context, 'Empowerment' could be defined as "a process that enhances ability of disadvantaged (powerless individuals) groups to challenge and change (in their favour) existing power relationships that placed them in subordinate economic, social and political position". Empowerment can manifest itself in acts of individual resistance as well as in group mobilization. Entitling women with land on the one hand, empower them economically on the other hand. Strengthen their ability to challenge social and political gender inequalities i.e., land rights would enhance women's 'freedom to achieve' or 'capability to function' in non-economic spheres as well.[12]

Prasad, Hemalatha (1998) of the National Institute of Rural Development, Hyderabad carried out two case studies, one in Salem district of Tamil Nadu and another in the Tribal Development Project areas of Andhra Pradesh to understand the process of economic empowerment of women. In Salem district 11 blocks were covered under International Fund for Agricultural Development Programme (IFAD). This project broadly envisaged empowering rural women by expanding their resources, improving access to credit, raising the level of awareness, better access to health and establishment of a viable model for women's development.[13]

Srnivasan, Girija and Satish (1999) in their study on impact of SHG lending on the profitability of branches studied eight branches where the SHG lending constituted more than five per cent of the loan portfolio. They concluded that lending to SHGs and NGOs carried the least cost when compared with other models of lending. Lending through SHGs reduced the costs by 85 per cent and through a federation, reduced the costs by 95 per cent as compared to direct lending. The default risk was negligible in the case of lending to SHG and NGO/federation.[14]

Beteille, Andre (1999) remarks that, the idea of empowerment has taken a hold over the minds of increasing number of persons in the last few years. It is now widely employed in the press, on television, and in political, academic and even legal circles. There is talk about the empowerment of the poor, of backward communities, of women and of various other disadvantaged sections of society. Empowerment is seen by many politicians, publicists, social activists and a growing section of the intelligentsia generally as the only effective answer to oppression, exploitation, injustice and the other maladies with which our society is beset. The idea of empowerment contains exciting possibilities. The first thing to note is that there is very little guidance available in existing social theory on the idea of empowerment as it is currently used in public discussion in India.[15]

Singh, Kalar (1999) observes that an SHG is a small group of individual members who voluntarily come together and form an association for achieving a common objective. In most cases, SHGs are constituted by persons known to one another and coming from the same village, community, or neighbourhood. That is, SHGs are small in size with membership ranging from 10 to 25, are homogeneous and have certain pre-group social binding factors. The purpose for which SHGs are formed varies from managing a common pool of resources, such as an irrigation facility and free plantation on common land, to providing such basic amenities as a school, health centre and so on. In the context of micro-finance, SHGs are formed around the theme of savings and credit. Under the SHG-Bank Linkage Programme, three linkage models have broadly emerged. Under the first mode, banks are directly linked to SHGs without the intervention of the NGOs. In the second mode, banks are providing, credit to SHGs and NGOs act as Self-help Promoting Institutions (SHPIs). Under the third mode, NGOs are acting both as Self-Help promoting Institutions and financial intermediaries for channelising credit from banks to SGHs. As on 31 March 1997, the SHGs linked to banks under the three models numbered 1,105, 3,889 and 3,604 respectively, and the bank loans advanced to them were worth Rs.11.84 crore.[16]

Selvaraj, R. and G. Vasanthi (1999) observe that these SHGs, because of their manageable size, close knit identity and operational flexibility are fast emerging as promising instruments of job creation and income generation among rural youth. The basic needs of rural youth for starting self-employment ventures are finance and organizational help. Financial requirements of the SHG's members are very small. Poverty alleviation would be the immediate objective of promotion of self-employment in rural areas, the long term objective should be entrepreneurial development of rural youth. Through the SHG's lot of new micro-enterprises can be developed in rural areas. Development of micro-enterprises leads to poverty reduction.[17]

Basu, Sukumar (2000) observes that, women at present contribute to the promotion of economic development of a country in various capacities as they perform not only non-market activities through which they produce goods having greater "use-values", but also various market activities in field, factories, offices and elsewhere outside home. So the dual role of a woman: one, as a contributor to production in a country and the other, as a reproducer of human race have been emphasized in our literature.[18]

The National Bank for Agriculture and Rural Development (2000) conducted a study on the impact of Micro-finance (MF) on the living standards of SHG members. The study aimed to find out how far the SHG bank linkage programme had lightened the burden of life for the average member of a SHG and to analyse the betterment of household by gaining access to micro-finance. The study covered 560 SHG member households from 223 SHGs spread over

11 States. It showed positive results. There were perceptible and wholesome changes in the living standards of the SHG members, in terms of ownership of assets, increase in savings and borrowing capacity, income generating activities and income levels. The study revealed that almost all the members developed saving habits in the post SHG situation as against 23 per cent of households increasing savings from Rs.4,282 to Rs.8,341. The study concluded that the involvement in the group significantly contributed to improving the self-confidence of the members. The feelings of self-worth and communication with others improved after association with the SHGs and the members were relatively more assertive in confronting social evils and problem situations. As a result, there was a fall in the incidence of family violence.[19]

Sen, Mahab (2000) has attempted a study to find out the development of SHGs promoted by Sreemamahiala Samity and its impact on women members. It was a study of 10 SHGs selected in Nadia district on a random sampling technique in July, 1999. The study included focus group discussion with the members of the SHGs in separate sessions followed by interview of 100 members through structured schedule. The findings of the study revealed that the individual loans were mostly used for productive purposes, the rate of recovery was very high compared to the rate of recovery of the formal institutional system and group dynamics was an instrument for change in the quality of life of the poor people. The study also revealed that other than economic activities, the groups worked towards primary education, basic health care of family, safe drinking water and environment protection. The study concluded that group cohesion, group action, need-based credit timely repayment are essential elements for sustainability of the groups.[20]

The study under review was a case study on "Empowerment of women through NGOs – The SEWA Bank experience". This study was done by Suman Jain (2000). The study observed that the bank SEWA (Self-employed

Women's Association) had been providing banking services to the poor, illiterate, self employed women and had become a viable financial venture. The case study revealed that there were 67113 women depositors with a working capital of Rs.1916.72 lakh in 1966. It further observed that the banks helped the women to acquire skills to make new products and identify work opportunities. It is also found that the repayment rate has been excellent, which was between 93 and 96 per cent due to close monitoring by the bank, the link between the group leaders and borrowers and constant communication between the bank and village groups. The conclusion was that from the women's point, their involvement in and ownership of a successful institution enhanced their collective strength and empowerment that came with organisation. From a wider perspective, member-owned or controlled micro-credit institution could help to strengthen the country's democratic system.[21]

Kallur, M.S., and Biradar, A.A. (2000) in their micro-level study aimed to examine the role of non-governmental voluntary organizations in promoting the micro-credit institutions and to comment on their sustainability in the years to come. The study was based on secondary data. The study has thrown light on the origin and the nature of micro-credit organization and its superiority over macro ones in catering to the need of farmers. It also revealed that as a result of continuous efforts of NABARD, 255 groups linked together as on 31st March 1998. This increased to 14,317 covering 30 commercial banks, 101 RRBs (Regional Rural Banks), 17 co-operative banks, 260 NGOs in 19 states and two union territories involving bank loans of Rs. 23.62 crore and NABARD refinance of Rs. 21.38 crore. The study also discussed the role of micro-credit organisations with particular reference to the Indo-Swiss project and their sustainability and concluded that the NGOs have succeeded in promoting SHGs.[22]

Manimekalai, N. (2000) in her study on "NGO's intervention through Micro-credit for Self-Help Women

Groups in Rural Tamil Nadu" had attempted to analyse the working of the SEVAI (Society of Education Village Action and Improvement) in empowering women and the rural poor through micro-credit. The objectives of the study were to find out the characteristics and working of the micro-credit institution namely, Viluthukal. This was a bank established for the benefit of SHGs to assist them by extending micro-credit and to highlight the strategies adopted to mobilize the women to form Self-Help Groups. The study was based on primary and secondary data. The secondary data were collected from the records of SEVAI and the primary data were collected from 70 women who were the members and who had availed credit from the bank. The analysis of the study revealed that the women in rural areas were really longing for supplementary income and the intervention through micro-credit, by both government, non-government organizations, would be a boon to them. The study also proved that, after the micro-credit and intervention of SEVAI, the education of the children has been better cared for and the women beneficiary households were able to manage the budget without deficit. The study concluded with the suggestion that micro-credit strategies could be followed by other institutions working for the upliftment of women and prove that micro-credit would be instrumental in realizing the proposed objectives.[23]

Karmaker, K.G. (1999-2000) remarks that the London-based Bames Institute carried out a study (May 1990) in 11 countries, including India, providing that the poor are credit-worthy if credit can be channelled to enterprising individuals and small groups through non-banking organizations. Credit schemes are founded on the basis of solidarity and loans are given to individuals in a group, who are also borrowers and act as co-guarantors for loans. NGOs besides facilitating the creation of SHGs also discuss a whole range rural problems, including social, political and personal.[24]

Choudhury, R.C., and Mohan, N. (2001) conducted a study to document the experience of SHGs in promoting micro-enterprises through micro-credit interventions and the efficacy of Self-Help Promoting Institution (SHPI). The study analysed the core issue of poverty reduction and efficacy of SHG route micro-enterprise promotion. The main objectives of the study were to analyse the operating systems in SHGs, to explore the effectiveness of SHGs in identifying the micro-enterprises and to suggest appropriate policy intervention for effective performance of SHGs. The study was carried out in selected clusters spread over regions in the states of Tamil Nadu, Karnataka, Andhra Pradesh and Maharashtra. The study covered 76 SHGs, 450 members and 135 micro-entrepreneurs from five regions. The case study-cum-survey method was followed. Secondary data were also collected from the records of SHGs. It was observed that group enterprise on a big scale would involve greater risks but would yield better returns to the entrepreneurs. The study brought to the fore the fact that, out of three SHPIs namely, NGOs, banks and government, NGOs were better equipped for capacity building of SHGs and promotion of micro-enterprises. The study also showed that SHGs were still in a state of flux and their sustainable development depended on a number of factors which were internal and external to the organisation.[25]

Namboodiri, N.V., and R.L. Shiyani (2001) conducted a study to find out the basic features and financial operations of SHGs promoted by both SHPI and NGOs served by the Panchmahals Vadodara Grameen Bank (PVGB). A sample of five branches of PVGB were selected, out of which three are located in Dahod district and two in panchmahals district, Gujarat. The main findings that emerged from this study were that, while the percentage of women groups promoted by the SHPI was 52 per cent, it was as high as 84 per cent for those promoted by the NGOs. The percentage of SHGs linked by the SHPI was 65 per cent and that of NGO was 42 per cent. The average amount advanced to SHGs varied from

Rs.7,000 to Rs.30,000 for those promoted by the NGOs. The SHG that were promoted by the NGOs had a better saving performance compared to that of SHPI, in terms of amount saved per SHGs as well as in terms of credit saving ratio. The repayment performance of the SHGs promoted by the SHPI was superior to that of NGOs.[26]

Dadhich, C.L., (2001) conducted a case study of Oriental Bank Grameen Project at Dehradun District in Uttar Pradesh, for assessing the benefit of the project and economic viability. Out of a total 450 SHGs covered by the project, 447 were women groups and only 3 were men SHGs. The main findings of the study revealed that a large number of women had taken up subsidiary occupations and consequently their family incomes had substantially increased. An analysis of figures relating to income and expenditure of a specialized micro-credit branch revealed that the branch had become a profit-centre right in the second year of its operation. The recovery of the loans was more than 100 per cent of the demand. The study also revealed that the borrowers under Oriental bank Grameen Project had both the advantages of the rate of interest, as well as hassle – free credit, whereas their counterparts elsewhere were paying exorbitant rates of interest.[27]

The objective of the Madheswaran, S., and Dharmadhikary Amita's (2001) study on "Empowering Rural Women Through SHGs" was to examine the SHG mechanism of the micro-credit scheme as an effective and financially viable tool in channelising credit to the rural poor. In this study an attempt has been made to analyse the impact of SHGs in providing credit to rural women, to help them to uplift their economic status. The analysis was based on a survey of three villages of Pune district, conducted during 1999, where the Maharashtra Rural Credit Programme was being implemented. The study revealed that the Maharashtra Rural Credit Programme was successful to some extent in its objective due to a combination of factors such as (i) SHG-Bank linkage, (ii) Credit being made available for consumption purposes, (iii) easy and periodic availability of credit due to rotation of savings, (iv) active participation of the NGOs. The study further revealed that peer monitoring could be used as a channel to provide credit at a low transaction cost and frequently to reduce rural poverty. The study concluded that micro-credit should be used to meet the current demands of the rural women and this would lead to a gradual improvement in the quality of their life and would enable them to identify activities for economic betterment.[28]

Satish, P. (2001) in his study made an attempt to answer the following questions (i) Are there a large number of pre existing groups in the rural areas and if so can they evolve into suitable SHGs? (ii) Are the really poor accepted as members of SHGs? (iii) What are the processes in SHG formation? (iv) Do the SHGs face resistance at the time of their formation, if so how is the resistance being overcome? This study covered groups formed by the NGOs and banks. The number of groups formed by the NGOs and banks were five and four respectively in Karnataka, four and nil in Maharashtra and seven and two in Uttar Pradesh. These groups were selected for the study. The secondary data and material were collected over the period 1997 to 2000 at the Bankers Institute of Rural Development (BIRD, Lucknow). The study revealed that several SHGs included very poor members and the process of SHG formation had to be systematic whether it was formed by a bank or an NGO. It also observed that most of the SHGs had faced initial resistance in their efforts. The study concluded that the NGOs were more suited for forming and nurturing the SHGs.[29]

The National Institute of Bank Management (NIBM, 2001) has studied SHGs in four districts of Maharashtra promoted under Maharashtra Rural Credit Project (MRCP). The study observed that 69 per cent of the groups were of the size 11-20, 50 per cent of the members were illiterate. The study further observed that 55 per cent of the office bearers had at least a secondary level of education. The study revealed that the average savings of the SHGs in MRCP was Rs. 24 per month per member. This rate was more for new groups than for the old groups. The study also found that the average amount of savings mobilized amounted to Rs.10658 per group and that the SHGs in MRCP had started lending their own thrift from the eighth month of their formation.[30]

Veluraj, R. (2001) remarks that the nobel scholar and Indian economist Mr. Amartya K. Sen expressed in his words,

> "Unless women are re empowered issues like literacy, health, population explosion will remain unresolved problems of developing countries".

In India, the majority of the women still continue to perform their traditional roles in the household and in agriculture. The women are the wives of men and the present scenario forces them to depend on men. Representation of women has never gone beyond eight per cent in Parliament, 10 per cent in the State Assemblies, 13 per cent in Council of Ministers, and 5.8 per cent in senior management and administrative posts of government and hence there is no equal opportunity. Women are more efficient than men, sometimes, they contribute a lot to the economic development. In particular self-help groups are the central activity which would result in social and economic development. SHGs also facilitated to achieve independence in their lives. Further, SHGs helped to improve their mental ability through proper education. The SHGs of Grameen Banks of Bangladesh and Self Employed Women Association (SEWA) are the examples of successful SHGs in Bangladesh and India respectively.[31]

Shrivastava, R.S. and Abha Avasthi (2001) observes that, there has been some serious discussion in India about the nature and mode of women empowerment as a means of dealing with various problems of women. Though the concept itself is far from clear, it means empowering women socially, economically and politically so that they can break away from male domination and claim equality with them. The various approaches towards women's empowerment could be articulated through a variety of theoretical perspectives. Some of these are the perspectives of critical theory, feminism and Marxism. Women are generally marginalized, under represented and depicted in a hierarchical and stereotyped imagery of the sexes. It is from this point of view that the media in contemporary society plays a crucial role in the construction and reconstruction of 'maleness' and 'femaleness' as cultural symbols. In devising various strategies for women's empowerment one view upholds their equality with men. It is argued that if women are given equal rights with men, their problems can be solved. Several women's activist movements are directed towards this end. Their condition can be improved only if they could enjoy equal rights with men.[32]

Lalitha, N., and B.S. Nagarajan (2002) conducted a critical study on the functioning of the SHGs in selected districts of Tamil Nadu. The study was undertaken to document the efforts of NGOs in promoting SHGs. The objectives of the study were to trace the structure and modalities of Self-help groups, study the functioning of the SHGs, examine the role of SHG in promoting empowerment of women, investigate the group dynamics of SHGs, identify the factors which contributed to the success / failure of the groups and study the income generating programmes promoted by SHGs. The study was based on multistage sampling technique. It had been carried out in three districts. NGOs who had organized SHGs for more than four years were identified. Out of 14 institutions, nine NGOs were selected and two SHGs from each NGO were selected on the basis of non-proportionate random sampling method. The study was based on survey method and had covered both secondary and primary data. The study highlighted the facts that SHGs were people's institutions and with their support, the women could march towards empowerment and that the groups could promote individual and group ventures of income generating activities under the effective guidance of NGOs. The study also revealed that effective leadership, group cohesiveness, savings, regular meetings, peer group pressure, linkage with other institutions and effective supervision by the NGOs were the factors which contributed to the success of the groups.[33]

Sudha Rani, K.D., *et.al.*, (2002) had undertaken a study to evaluate the social status of women in house management, leadership qualities, health and sanitation and economic status after participation in the Self-Help Groups. Out of 600 Self-help groups established by Padmavathi Mahila Mandal, tirupathi, Andhra Pradesh, 50 Self-help groups were randomly selected for the study. From each group selected, two women members were selected randomly. The study was based on primary data and a specially designed rating scale was administered to the sample to collect the information. The findings of the study revealed that, in all the four aspects there was positive correlation between the women's education status and empowerment. The study observed that the participation in SHGs enhanced the empowerment of women in these four aspects. Self-confidence among the women increased. Their decision-making power also increased during the period of participation.[34]

In order to make micro-finance a more effective tool in future issues such as over dependence of MFI's on local community savings, resource mobilization from domestic and international markets, development of prudential norms, accounting system, diversification of products, ratings, involvement of local bodies and policy implications, it requires specific focus in times to come. Various components of existing Government of India schemes, targeted for eradication of poverty such as SJSRY, VMBY, NSDP etc., need to be carefully integrated with suitable micro-finance mechanisms and city production system to achieve the desired success in eradication of povert (Kumar, 2009).[35]

Micro-finance programmes have dealt a definite impact on poverty with measurable changes in various socio-economic parameters namely, children's education (including the girl child), nutritional and health status and women's participation in decision making particularly at the household level.

There is a need to nurture and build micro-finance institutions, which would provide timely access to micro-finance services at reasonable cost and on a permanent basis. There is a definite requirement to invest time, effort and funds for capacity building of NGOs and emerging MFIs in an attempt to expand the outreach and impact of micro-finance institutions (Mane and Asthana, 2004).[36]

We can conclude that it would be most unwise to assume that the SHGs in Jabalpur, either those few which exist now or the larger numbers which we must hope will emerge in future, are strictly equitable, either in their membership or in the distribution of benefits among the members. Inequality persists, within the nation, the states, the districts, the villages and even within the few SHGs which are in each village. This is not because of any evil genius of the Indian people, nor of the population of Madhya Pradesh or Jabalpur, but is the result of the tendency that Marx observed, the rich get richer and the poor get poorer. We must search for the constraints to equity at every level, and try in every way possible to reverse the trend (Harper and Nath, 2004)[37]

The micro-finance sector in India has grown significantly in the last one decade with the participation of NGOs, MFIs and private sector, as the formal financial institutions have reduced their outreach after reforms in the 1990s. The micro-finance sector, particularly the SHG-bank linkage program appears to have the potential of becoming a big success. However, inadequate investment in capacity building is the important constraint that hinder the growth of the micro-finance sector. There is emergence of good capacity building institutions. These institutions focus on training staff of MFIs or mainstream financial institutions. However, there are now close to a million SHGs in India, which require capacity building in comparison with micro-credit demand. Several studies have shown significant impact on the livelihoods of poor due to micro-finance (Mahajan and Kumar, 2004).[38]

To be successful, financial intermediaries that provide services and generate domestic resources must have the capacity to meet high performance standards. They must achieve excellent repayments and provide access to clients. And they must build towards operational and financial self-sufficiency and increasing client reach. In order to do so, micro-finance institutions need to find ways to cut down on their administrative costs and also to broaden their resource base. Standardizing the operational procedures with effective control systems through simplified and decentralized loan application approval and collection process, for instance, through group loans which give borrowers responsibilities for much of the loan application process, allow the loan officers to handle many more clients and hence reduce costs (Udaia Kumar 2004).[39]

Under its Swanirvar project scheme, Bagaria Relief and Welfare Ambulance Society charges 24 per cent rate of interest on loans and pays 5 per cent on deposits. It receives funds from the bank (UBI) at about 12 per cent rate of interest. Operating expenses for the Swanirvar project during the year ending March 2003 amounted to about Rs.1.16 lakh. For the previous year, the figure was Rs.1.05 lakh. Given the mid-year loan size of about Rs.6.63 lakh for the Swanirvar (i.e. non-SGSY) project and mid-year total savings of about Rs. 10.15 lakh for the same project in the year ended 2003, this translates to a transaction cost of 6.90 per cent of combined loans and deposits (17.46 per cent loans alone and 11.40 per cent of deposits only). For the previous year the mid-year loan figure was about Rs.6.26 lakh and the mid-year deposit figure was about Rs.8.94 lakh. Thus costs amounted to 6.93 per cent of combined loans and savings (16.81 per cent of loans alone and 11.78 per cent of deposits only). For the year 2002-2003, the recovery rate has been about 95 per cent, which is quite commendable. Historically the figure has always been higher than 95 per cent. Given the considerable size of the organization and the scale of its operations, this is a commendable performance (Chakrobarti, 2004).[40]

All the past attempts to provide the poor with easy access to formal savings and credit have had limited success. Going by the experience so far the prospects for the poor to obtain their due share in the final finance appear relatively better under the linkage programme. But the programme still has a very long way to go if it has to become the core strategy of the banking sector. The response of financial institutions to the programme in general has been very tardy. All the key stakeholders need to take stock of their experiences and make a concerted effort on the lines pointed above to take the programme forward. The key to the success lies in retaining the basic character and strength of SHGs along with integrating them appropriately with outside systems to meet the needs of the members in an enduring way. What is needed for its future success is a highly co-ordinated effort among all the stakeholders at different levels (Shylendra, 2004).[41]

In spite of the commendable achievements Kerala could make in the social sector, the women of the state have only secondary status in society. However, since the inception of Kudumbashree, the scenario has been changing dramatically. Women empowerment is a major concern and prime priority activity for the mission. Every activity of the project is geared to take the beneficiary towards this ultimate goal. Weekly meetings, discussions, thrift and credit operations, participation in planning and implementation process of development activities and social and cultural activities conducted under the aegis of Kudumbashree CBOs enhance the confidence and capacity of poor women. Moreover, thrift and credit operations and micro-enterprises have alleviated the economic status of the poor women in families and society.

It is an unarguable fact that Kudumbashree Mission and its activities, including the planned capacity building exercise of the beneficiaries, have really improved the status of poor women in the urban and rural areas of the State (Jose, 2004).[42]

Micro-entrepreneurs under SJSRY may find it difficult to compete with the city production system in terms of quality, pricing and marketing strategies. Therefore Urban Self-employment Programme (USEP) needs to be integrated with city production system by involving local level business, industry and trade for the provision of non-financial services such as training, technology transfer, wage employment, marketing skills etc. The expansion scope of micro-finance under SJSRY is fairly wide and essential to achieve the national policy objective to become a developed nation by the year 2020. In this process of socio-economic transformation, cities and the urban poor have to play a central role for enhancement of overall productivity through a well-designed strategy of local economic development (Panday, 2004).[43]

This is where marketing MFI debt to market could play an important role. There is a subsidy element in soft loans. It is the difference between the interest rate of the soft loan and rate that MFIs would have to pay to borrow the funds commercially from the money markets. For example, if the interest rate payable on a soft loan is two per cent a year, and the money market rate for the same amount of funds is 14 per cent (not uncommon in poor countries), then the element of subsidy in the soft loan would be 12 per cent a year. Conceptually, it is the equivalent of a grant from the lender of the soft loan, and the MFI should get credit for this, capitalising in on the balance sheet as equips like any other grant. The market value of the loan is determined by discounting the cash flows during the loan term, both principal and interest, by the commercial rate of debt. The difference between the present value of the debt cash flows and the amount of loan funding received is equal to the grant. As the loan moves closer to maturity, the amount of the debt obligation will rise while the grant component declines (Gibbons, 2004).[44]

Micro-credit programmes go a long way in achieving women's empowerment and economic self-sufficiency. In micro-financing schemes women form self-help groups, define their priorities as a collective and obtain access to credit and information for self-employed opportunities. Self-help groups are accepted as critical actors in helping women to achieve economic independence and stability. Micro-credit substantially paves the way for women's empowerment. Self-reliance, self-confidence and self-esteem are strengthened by self-help groups. The women's Self-Help Group is a movement in itself. Women who have never stepped out from within the four walls of their homes converge to form small bands of saving groups in an effort to confront the looming problem of access to credit for taking minimal care of their family needs (Basu, 2004).[45]

Development NGOs are community builders first and foremost. In micro-finance for poverty reduction, however, it has also been evident that institutional innovations sustained poverty reduction. In this sense, success cannot and should not be measured without reference to goals that include impacts that are both immediate and long-term. Charity is not a foundation on which anything more than relief can be built. (Rhyne, 2001). 'Welfare' approach to micro-finance and MED does not sit well with sustainability, growth in self-reliance, or the priorities and commercial practices approved by the many donor agencies that are ready, willing and able to fund micro-finance activities. If access to donor funds for these purposes is a goal, the welfare approach to micro-finance is not appropriate and will very likely do clients a serious disservice. Access to mainstream financial services must be assumed to be at commercial rates. If the clients that an NGO serves come off programmes that are provided at subsidized rates, it will be all the more difficult for them to migrate or graduate into the commercial mainstream. Hence, if mainstream clients entering into existing financial systems is a goal, strategies have to be adopted that will remove any dependence that clients may have on subsidies, poorly designed products and services, or practices that do not enable poor households to achieve levels of self-reliance typical among households able to keep themselves above the poverty line (Remenji, 2004).[46]

Experience indicates that a number of factors are important to successful micro-finance partnerships (Malaugblin, 2004):[47]

- active commitment from top management to front line staff;
- leadership that encourages, supports and rewards staff performance consistent with effective partnership relationships;
- knowledgeable and interpersonally skilled staff who can build team spirit and bridges within your organization and with partners;
- willingness to learn and to change practices when necessary for the success of the partnership;
- open discussion of partnership challenges, allowing staff to resolve and even predict difficulties;
- collaboration in planning, problem solving, monitoring and evaluation;
- agreements and relationship that transcend individuals mean that staffing changes won't interrupt or jeopardize operations; and
- long-term commitment to partnership acknowledges that it takes three to five years to build a sustainable programme and anticipates benefits that will continue long after the formal agreement is concluded.

Through linkage with commercial banks, Thrift & Credit Societies (TCS) have undertaken intermediation between the bank and their members earning profit and building a stronger corpus of funds for further lending. A number of TCS conduct regular meetings and organize cultural activities such as, kirtans etc., and celebrate national and other festivals.

Gupta, S.K. (2004)[48] Observes some of the Project Officers, District Urban Development Agency (DUDA) have reported that there is a fall in the application of micro-project under Urban Self-Employment Programme (USEP) component of SISRY and also a corresponding rise in application for formation of group economic activities under Development of Women and Children in Urban Areas (DWCUA).

Sharma, R.H. (2002)[49] observes that, in recent years, often at the behest of non-governmental organizations, public welfare agencies have begun to allow experiments and demonstration projects, waiving assets and income limitations for some low-income entrepreneurs and allowing them to participate in micro-credit programmes. There is growing awareness that very poor people are ready and willing to pull themselves out of poverty if given access to basic economic inputs. This insight has led to growing support for micro-credit programmes that serve the very poor in urban neighbourhoods and in rural areas. Any new idea is only old wine in the new bottle.

As stated by Lalitha N. and B.S. Nagarajan (2002)[50] Empowerment literally means 'becoming powerful'. Empowerment of rural poor demands that members of village communities should have their own organizations which will serve their own economic needs and interests exclusively. Moreover sufficient knowledge about the needs and problems of rural poor have not been supplied to the policy-making agencies. If SHGs are promoted the group members can articulate the problems in a better manner.

Banerjee, G.D. (2002)[51] observes that the participation of women in SHGs made a significant impact on their empowerment both in social and economic aspects. Most of the women were able to increase their income level manifold and contributed to the development of their family. In the process, many of the women reported that they were participating in the financial decisions of the family, which earlier they were not allowed to do. The members were getting support from their husbands, which was not available before they joined the group. Women members expressed full satisfaction over their performance and wanted to continue their association with the groups. It is quite heartening to see that in one men's group, all the members decided to keep away from alcohol. If any member violated the decision he was expelled from the group and his dues from the group was withheld. Similarly, many women could successfully check the liquor types of family problems. Most of the members were sending their children to school. It was quite interesting to observe that a few women members of the groups got elected in panchayat bodies. The group dynamism helped the women to pressurize the authorities in laying of roads, getting electric connections and providing drainage, borewell and constructing community halls. Women are coming out in the open to discuss their common problems, which would not have been possible in the absence of such group activities. This type of social impact would definitely go a long way in improving the quality of life of the members.

Singh, Sudat (2004)[52] in his article presents the findings of an empirical study of the elected women representatives of the Panchayat Raj Institutions of Haryana for exploring the extent of their empowerment as a result of the implementation of the 73rd Amendment to the Indian Constitution which made provision for the reservation of one-third share for women in these institutions. It also aims at making some suggestions for making the participation of women effective in these institutions of decentralized rural governance.

Singh, Naresh (2004)[53] explains the critical analysis of the emergence and growth of micro-finance sector in Bangladesh and India reflects that initially micro-finance projects were started from the micro-enterprise projects. The micro-finance sector has grown at a very fast rate in both the countries. Over a period of time the growth of the sector in both the countries reflects certain similar patterns. The four approaches of micro-finance discussed in this paper along with their case examples show that micro-finance has made impact on the life of people, strengthened the capabilities of poor people to start income generating activities/micro-enterprises. The recovery rate is very high under micro-finance projects, which reflects the economic and financial sustainability of the projects. Innovations are being accepted under micro-finance sector. Thus micro-insurance has emerged as an important innovation in both the countries. Bangladesh and India being poor countries, entire development strategy should be pro-poor through micro-finance with the active support of Governments.

Pal, Mahi (2004)[54] in his article discusses the social development status of women particularly in term of their general health and nutrition, sex ratio, education and physical quality because these aspects of their development are very necessary for their empowerment and capacity building as reproductive and productive actors in Indian society and economy.

Soundadapandian, M. (2001)[55] suggests that linkages between banks and Self-Help Groups (SHGs) can have either direct or indirect impact on rural credit systems. Banks can make available credit to SHGs which, in turn, can make credit available to their members. Alternatively, banks can work through a voluntary organization, which can provide credit to SHGs to be passed on to the members. The route chosen by banks will depend upon the strength of the SHGs. Banks with VOs have always proved beneficial.

Jha, T.N. (2002)[56] observes that the micro-finance models in Bangladesh, despite a few weaknesses, demonstrated a number of strong positive attributes. With restricted outreach of the formal credit agencies in India, micro-finance models of Bangladesh do offer a few lessons to us in our efforts to tackle the twin problems of mass poverty and unemployment. In a nutshell, it can be concluded that the micro-finance models in Bangladesh, despite a few weaknesses, demonstrated a number of strong positive attributes in terms of operational simplicities, better accessibilities, wider outreaches, emphasis on women empowerment and availability of a wide range of credit and non-credit services.

Amutha, R. (2006) finds the following in his study. Of the sample, respondents belong to SC – the most economically oppressed class is more. It could be observed from the analysis that middle age group's involvement is higher than the young and old age group's involvement. It is found from the analysis that the majority of the respondents have completed school education. It could be observed from the analysis that the majority members have medium size families. From the analysis it is found that most of the respondents are employed as casual labourers followed by domestic workers.

This study by Usha Mandhini and Padma Rani (2006)[58] clearly concludes the role of micro-finance on the rural women. Now-a-days women's participation in managing the family is higher than male members. These arrangements nowadays trash out the inferiority feelings of the women members. Moreover participation of rural women in SHG improves the decision-making empowerment of women, improved the standard of living of the rural poor, and as women became economically independent they will gain greater social standing in the household, and in the village.

Their activities like offering help for inter caste marriages, raising voice against illegal drugs, solved many social problems. They were equally treated with men in all the activities. SHGs give a hand to the rural people in a positive way to lead their life; also some kind of relaxation from tension can be seen around them. During the study confidence and determination along with absence of caste feelings among them was identified from their face.

Dasgupta, Rajaram (2001) explains that the government instead is required to create an environment where genuine NGOs can perform effectively as SHPIs and banks can conduct business with SHGs on their own. The right type of incentives for banks in terms of grading, income-tax benefit, performance appraisal and reward and punishment, etc., are the better tools and should be tried first. Government can promote SHPIs in NGO-lacking regions through well-established and well-accepted SHPIs, and continuation of support depending upon their performance. Banks, on the other hand, should be left free to evaluate SHPIs and SHGs for conducting business with them. The subsidy amount may be used for infrastructure, training, backward and forward linkages and other requirements of the poor, not the poor-borrowers alone. All these are likely to improve the opportunity for investment by the poor. Simultaneously, the poor will improve their savings potential, credit-handling capacity and access to financial institutions, inculcate entrepreneurial skill, develop an urge for investment credit facility. Government needs to ensure adequate flow of credit to the poor according to their needs and facilitate opportunities of income generation. Along with monitoring mandatory credit, government needs to monitor efficacy of the credit through appropriate tools. The SHGs should be considered as one of the best means to counter social and financial exclusion and enhance economic, political and social citizenship not an end in itself.

The SHGs were able to provide various credit services such as business loan, consumption loan, loan for settlement of old debt and loan for other contingency purposes to their members. The SHGs under study are characterized by heterogeneity in terms of social and economic indicators. The principle of self-selection by members in order to have social cohesiveness of the group which is widely discussed in the theoretical literature, is indirectly reinforced as members of SHGs were drawn from the Integrated Child Development Programme target families sponsored by the Central and State Governments. The success of SHGs in terms of high repayment is mostly related to the exploitation of prevailing social ties and social cohesion found among women members. Social cohesiveness among members spring not only from their diverse background of knowledge base, skills, occupations and income levels, but also due to the dynamic incentive system of progressive lending to the groups on the successful completion of loan repayment. However, SHGs are heavily dependent on external financial agencies for their lending operations. While it is not possible to achieve self-sufficiency of SHGs given their socio-economic status of members, a greater thrust should be given to internal resource mobilization for viable and sustainable business operations in future (Datta and Ramon, 2001).[60]

Mamboodiri and Shiyani (2001) observes that one of the major weaknesses of the SHGs is that they limited the scope for future growth in membership. Second, the loan portfolio is dominated by consumption loan and hence there is limited opportunity for income generating activities. Since women groups exclusively dominate the SHGs, their empowerment both in economic and social fronts is one of the great opportunities, particularly for women, to participate in the mainstream of development activities. Opportunities for earnings through deposits and higher off-farm income opportunities improve their disposable income. For the banks the SHGs are better financial intermediaries. One of the major threats is that the SHGs do not have any legal status. Rapid expansion in the number of these groups without close monitoring by the sponsoring agencies may lead to their poor functioning. This is more so when they diversify their operations that need better management capabilities. To sum up, the system evolved through the SHGs for collective savings, group consumption credit, integrating social and economic goals among small groups has the potential not only for financial deepening in the rural areas but also for the empowerment of women in particular.

Several SHGs included very poor members but no conscious attempt was made by the promoters to include exclusively the poorest of a village while forming an SHG as they felt that only after the SHG concept has trickled down to the poorest strata of the village society, it was possible to organize them into groups. The process of SHG formation has to be systematic whether it is formed by a Bank or an NGO. The basic steps in pre-formation and post-formation are similar to both these agencies. However, due to their nearness to the people and flexibility of operations, the NGOs seem to be better equipped to undertake SHG formation. Most of the SHGs have faced initial resistance in their efforts, but with the perseverance of their members the resistance could be overcome. The SHG experiment has so far been successful in a few pockets of the country. But it is essential that this spreads throughout rural India. As the NGOs are more suited for forming and nurturing of the SHGs, it is essential to strengthen them and their resources so that they would increasingly undertake this work (Satish, 2001).[62]

The importance of micro-finance as an effective vehicle of alleviating poverty, especially in rural areas through the empowerment of women is now widely recognized. There are several methods of opening a micro-finance project. The successful experience of a public sector bank, without the involvement of either the Government or any non-government organization (NGO) in India is discussed here. Some suggestions for further improvement, based on the experience of certain other similar projects are also made (Dadhich, 2001).[63]

Madheswaran and Dharmadhikary, (2001) observes that major challenge for micro-credit scheme is the viability of non-farm economic activities. Two major problems are, firstly, to find an economic activity that will yield a rate of profit necessary to cover the interest rate on the loan. Secondly, marketing of the produce is a problem. The main market for non-farm activities is in the urban areas, hence, when these activities are taken up by rural women the produced goods cannot meet the standards of the urban market, the distance also increases the cost of marketing, which these women cannot bear. From the above it follows that micro-credit should be used to meet the current demands of the rural women, whether these are for health, education or consumption purposes. This will lead to a gradual improvement in the quality of their life and will enable them to identify activities for economic betterment. In this process they will learn fiscal discipline and be ready to take on market-oriented economic activities. For poverty alleviation and empowerment of women, intervention should be a continuous process, with intervention at a steady pace rather than with target-oriented intensive efforts at sporadic intervals. Apart from the agencies involved in implementing the MRCP, other departments like social welfare departments, tribal research centre, and local NGO may be involved to see whether the benefits of the programme are reaching the really needy people. This will be a more effective way of targeting the poorest of the poor.

Magnur *et al.*, (2005) explains in their study that the ability to generate income is a key element of socio-economic upliftment of families and thereby, the communities. Variety of different work and production activities are available that provide economic opportunities to rural women and such opportunities are labelled as micro-enterprises. In this context of lack of regular and remunerative wage employment, micro-enterprises represent opportunities for self-employment that the women can undertake with support of other family members.

The Micro-credit – SHGs model has got tremendous attention in recent years. Micro-credit is an alternative source of credit for the poor who earlier were considered as non-bankable. This system not only provides credit, most important input for development, to the poorer section of the society, but also aimed for their capacity building. It has also been observed that group lending has distinct advantage in the form of excellent recovery rate and improvement in income level. The phenomenal growth of SHGs indicates that the weaker sections of the society are also capable of sharpening their micro-entrepreneurial skills with the help of their own savings and additional bank credit, as needed. This point, micro-credit – SHGs integration could be the way out for overall rural development *vis-à-vis* poverty alleviation (Das, 2003).[66]

Dwarkanath, H.D. (2003) observes that Andhra Pradesh government has made a pioneering effort in community organization and monitoring the Self-Help Groups Action Plan in which rural women are largely involved. Women participation in the savings and credit movement has paved the way for the speedy development of economic and productive activities. This movement helped in bringing other institutions like commercial banks, NGOs and other micro-finance organisations for the upliftment of rural women. Another important factor which contributed towards the rapid expansion of savings and credit groups in Andhra Pradesh, is the collective participation of various organizations and credit institutions.

Women are at the receiving end of the adverse effects of economic development. Credit as a tool for organizing the poor, should be an entry point for larger social change. When the poor become stakeholders in development planning, they feel a sense of ownership for the programme. It is not the aspiration for empowerment, but factors like low income and unemployment which persuade them to start micro-enterprises, necessary to supplement the household income. Collectively, women stand to gain while individually they are vulnerable to various exploitative forces. Instead of the often repeated trickle-down theory, a 'bubble up' approach seems more appropriate. The main resource for broad-based rural development must come from the energy, ideas and determination of rural people themselves, from collective self-help to assisted self-reliance (Dubhashi, 2005).[68]

As a developing country, India faces constraints of resources for rapid socio-economic development. While there may be limitation of financial resources, available human resources are huge and yet to be fully exploited. Thus the major challenge before the nation today is to evolve appropriate strategy for mobilizing the human resources for optimising use of the available financial resources. Micro-finance provides a medium for ensuring this by optimising use of the financial resources. The task force on employment opportunities, while referring to the limitation of the formal financial system in meeting the credit needs of the informal sector, has underlined the importance of micro-finance through self-help groups as a potentially useful channel for generation of employment in the coming years. Notwithstanding the fact that the net incremental income to the beneficiaries availing micro-credit has been small, the noteworthy feature of micro-finance has been the confidence, managerial and entrepreneurial ability developed in the beneficiary, which enables them to take up any other economic activity in a viable manner. This makes the concept of micro-finance extremely important for a developing country. Once provision of micro-finance is tied up with support given under other schemes for training, acquisition of assets etc., the beneficiary will be able to increase income substantially, which will in turn be of great help in establishing an egalitarian society as envisaged in our constitution (Panda, 2003).[69]

Gadakar, H.H. (2005) said that the Mahila SHG Industrial Society aims at empowerment of women. It has facilitated marketing of their products and made them earn more income. Perhaps better marketing opportunities build confidence among women folk. The society has also taken care of 'Future' of its members by implementing LIC's Schemes. It has taken care of their children by extending scholarships. It also inculcates habit of thrift and saving through activities of banking counter and so on. It is because of the society's efforts, women empowerment has become a reality. Members are becoming self reliant. This visualizes the strength of women leadership in the cooperatives. If dynamic women leadership is encouraged in the field of cooperatives, this will strengthen cooperative development in all walks of life. The future aim of the society is to bring about overall development of its members through strengthening the SHG movement at grassroot level.[70]

Mishra, Chittadamjan (2005) observes two types of Self-Help Promoting Institutions (SHOI), namely, Government and NGOs are active in the household level garment sector. The DRD-Promoted SHGs are more organized and have better infrastructure to carry out the activities relating to the garment sector. The NGO-promoted SHGs, on the other hand, have taken part in other developmental activities in the village in a bigger way than in the DRD-promoted ones. The author is of the view that capacity building and credit availability are complementary inputs to the growth of SHG-based garment sector.

Opinions on the impact of micro-finance have been divided between those who see it as a "magic bullet" for women's empowerment and others who are dismissive of its abilities as a cure-all panacea for development. This paper seeks to examine the empirical evidence on the impact of micro-finance with respect to poverty reduction and empowerment of poor women. It becomes apparent that while access to financial services can and does make vital contributions to the economic productivity and social well-being of poor women and their households, it does not "automatically" empower women, just as with other interventions, such as education, political quotas, etc., that seek to bring about a radical structural transformation that true empowerment entails. These other interventions simply constitute different entry points into this larger project, each with the potential for social transformation, but each is contingent on context, commitment and capacity if this potential is to become a reality (Kabeer, 2005).[72]

In the context of bridging gaps in gender inequality, increasing attention is being paid to enable women to become active partners in decision-making, implementation and evaluation of all interventions initiated for energizing, organizing and sustaining their livelihoods. Experiences of NIRD action research projects reveal that, the operational aspects, such as, the extent of enabling that goes in the community self-help processes and sharpening of mind-set of women, men and the project administrators are two critical components that determine the extent to which empowerment, will or will not take place. The author, as the coordinator of action research projects, had direct field experiences and this article was developed on the basis of such first hand information. The NIRD action research groups by utilizing micro-credit as a main intervention have initiated a range of economic and social development activities and created positive impact on the status of women in their households and communities. In this context, an understanding of the process of empowerment is imperative for new theoretical development and practical applications by all those who are involved in improving the status of women and bridging gaps in gender inequalities. As on implication, it is preferable to devote more resources directly to facilitation and promotional components of empowerment process, rather than investing time and resources for justifying the failure of interventions at a later stage.[73]

It cannot be said that micro-credit can by itself promote economic growth. In reality, micro-credit is barely adequate even as an instrument for poverty alleviation, leave alone economic growth. To serve the purpose of economic growth, we need a new paradigm of livelihood finance with much larger levels of resource allocation, both from public resources as well as from the capital markets (C. Mahajan, 2005).[74]

SUMMARY

The above said reviews examined the concept of women's interest, concept of women's empowerment, micro-finance, working of micro-credit institutions and experience of SHGs in promoting micro-credit interventions. The present study focuses on an indepth analysis of performance of micro-finance and self-help groups.

REFERENCES

1. Schenk-Sandbergen, Loes, "Empowerment of Women in a Development Project", *Economic and Political Weekly*, Vol. XXVI, No. 7, April 27, 1991.
2. Hamsa, N., "Women in Economic Development Process", *Southern Economist*, Vol. 31, November 15, 1992.
3. Sinha, S.L.N., "Raising Women's Social Status", *Southern Economist*, Vol. 31, January 1, 1993.
4. Jain, R.K., "Economic Self-Reliance for Women", *Social Welfare*, February-March 1994.
5. Mohantry, Manoranjan, "On the Concept of Empowerment", Economic and Political Weekly, Vol.XXX, No.24, June 17, 1995.
6. Urvashi Gulati, "Development in India with Special Reference to Rural Women", *Kurukshetra*, August 1995.
7. Pinto, Marina, "Development Through Empowerment of Women in India", *Kurukshetra*, August 1995.
8. Puhazhendhi, V., "Transaction Costs of Lending to the Rural Poor – NGOs and SHGs of the Poor as Intermediaries for Banks in India", The Foundation for Development Corporation, Australia: Brisbane, 1995.
9. Indian Bank, "Performance of Indian Bank Branches in SHG Lending", *Rural Banker*, No. 21, 1995, p. 2.

10. Bankers Institute for Rural Development, "Bank Performance Improvement under Maharashtra Rural Credit Project", *Rural Banker*, No. 21, 1996, p. 22.

11. Sinha, S.L.N., *op. cit.*

12. Agarwal, Bina, A Field of One's Own, Cambridge University Press, 1998, p. 40.

13. Prasad, Hemalatha, "IFAD's (International Fund for Agricultural Development), Women's Development Programme for Economic Empowerment" In: Sushama Sahay (eds), *Women and Empowerment – Approaches and Strategies,* New Delhi: Discovery Publishing House, 1998, pp. 170-172.

14. Girija, Srinivasan and Satish, "Impact of SHG Lending on the Profitability of Branches", *Rural Banker*, No. 21, 1999, p. 22.

15. Beteille, Antre, "Empowerment", *Economic and Political Weekly*, Vol. XXXIV, Nos. 10 & 11, March 6-13, 1999.

16. Singh, Kalar, *Rural Development – Principles, Policies and Management*, Sage Publication, New Delhi, 1999, pp. 303 & 304.

17. Selvaraj, R., and Vasanthi, G., "Role of Self-Help Groups in Entrepreneurial Development", *The Tamil Nadu Journal of Cooperation,* June 1999.

18. Basu, Sukumar, *Women and Economic Development,* Deep & Deep Publication Pvt. Ltd., New Delhi, 2000, p. 100.

19. National Bank for Agriculture and Rural Development (NABARD), *Report on Impact of Micro-finance on the Living Standards of SHG Members,* 1999-2000, Mumbai.

20. Sen, Manab, "Self-Help Groups and Micro-Finance: An Alternative Socio Economic Option for the Poor", In: Kamta Prasad (eds.), *NGO's and Socio-Economic Development Opportunities,* New Delhi: Deep and Deep Publications Pvt. Ltd., 2000, pp. 77-89.

21. Jain, Suman, "Empowerment of Women through NGOs – The SEWA Bank Experience" In: Kamta Prasad (eds.), *NGO's and Socio-Economic Development Opportunities,* New Delhi: Deep and Deep Publications Pvt. Ltd., 2000, pp.112-119.

22. Kallur, M.S., and A.A. Biradar, "The New Paraidm of Micro-finance and the Role of Non-governmental Voluntary Agencies in its Promotion: A Few Reflections" In: Kamta Prasad (eds.), *NGO's and Socio-Economic Development Opportunities,* New Delhi: Deep and Deep Publications Pvt. Ltd., 2000, pp. 67-75.

23. Manimekalai, N., "NGO's Intervention through Micro-Credit for Self-Help Women Groups in Rural Tamil Nadu" In: Kamta Prasad (eds.), *NGO's and Socio-Economic Development Opportunities,* New Delhi: Deep and Deep Publications Pvt. Ltd., 2000, pp. 96-110.

24. Karmakar, K.G. "Rural Credit and Self-Help Groups", *Journal of Social and Management Science,* Vol.XXIX, No.1, April-June 2000.

25. Choudhury, R.C., and N. Mohan, "Micro-Enterprises Development and SHGs", *Micro-Credit for Micro-Enterprises*, Hyderabad: National Institute of Rural Development, 2001, pp. 89-143.

26. Namboodiri, N.V., and R.L. Shiyani, "Potential Role of SHGs in Rural Financial Deepening", *Indian Journal of Agricultural Economics,* Vol. 56, No. 3, July-September, 2001, pp. 401-405.

27. Dadhich, C.L., "Micro-finance – A Panacea for Poverty Alleviation: A Case Study of Oriental Grameen Project in India", *Indian Journal of Agricultural Economics,* Vol. 56, No. 3, July-September, 2001, pp. 419-420.

28. Madheswaran, S., and Amita Dharmadhikasy, "Empowering Rural Women through SHGs: Lessons from Maharashtra Rural Credit Project", *Indian Journal of Agricultural Economics*, Vol. 56, No. 3, July-September, 2001, pp. 398-400.

29. Satish, P., "Some Issues in the Formation of Self-Help Groups", *Indian Journal of Agricultural Economics,* Vol. 56, No. 3, July-September, 2001, pp. 410-416.

30. National Institute of Bank Management (NIBM), "Maharashtra Rural Credit Project (MRCP)", *Indian Journal of Agricultural Economics,* Vol. 56, No. 3, July-September, 2001, pp. 400-402.

31. Veluraj, R., "Self-Help Groups – An Alternative Approach to Empower Rural Women", *The Tamil Nadu Journal of Cooperation,* June 2001.

32. Shrivastava, R.S. and Abha Avasthi, *Modernity, Feminism and Women Empowerment,* Rawat Publications, Jaipur and New Delhi, 2001, pp. 171-179.

33. Lalitha, N., and B.S. Nagarajan, "Functioning of the SHGs in Selected Districts of Tamil Nadu" (eds.), *Self-Help Groups in Rural Development,* New Delhi: Dominant Publishers and Distributors, 2002.

34. Sudha Rani, K., D. Umadevi and G. Surendra "SHGs, Micro-Credit and Empowerment", *Social Welfare*, February, 2002, pp. 20-22.

35. Rajan Kumar, *Issues in Microfinance, Shelter, Human Settlement Management Institute*, Vol..VII, No. 1, January 2004, p. 4.

36. Mane, Rahul and Rajiv Asthana, *Indian Experience in Micro-finance – An Overview, Shelter,* Human Settlement Management Institute, Vol. VII, No. 1, January 2004, pp. 10-11.

37. Harper, Malcolm and Dr. Manoj Nath, *Inequity in the Self-Help Group Movement – A View From India's Centre,* Shelter, Human Settlement Management Institute, Vol. VII, No. 1, January 2004, p. 22.

38. Mahajan, Vijay and L. Kumar, *Micro-finance in India – Development and Challenges,* Shelter, Human Settlement Management Institute, Vol. VII, No. 1, January 2004, p. 30.

39. Udaia Kumar, M., *Branding Micro-finance,* Shelter, Human Settlement Management Institute, Vol. VII, No. 1, January 2004, p. 34.

40. Chakrabarti, Rajesh, *Micro-finance in Eastern India – A Case Study,* Shelter, Human Settlement Management Institute, Vol. VII, No. 1, January 2004, p. 36.

41. Shylendra, H.S., *The Way Forward for SHG-Bank Linkage Programmes, Shelter,* Human Settlement Management Institute, Vol. VII, No. 1, January 2004, p. 43.

42. Jose, T.K., an Krishnakumar, K., Kudumbashree – *Poverty Reduction through Micro-Finance, Micro-Enterprise & Women Empowerment, Shelter,* Human Settlement Management Institute, Vol. VII, No. 1, January 2004, p. 51.

43. Panday, K.K., *Micro-Finance: Global Pattern and Lessons for Indian Initiatives,* Shelter, Human Settlement Management Institute, Vol. VII, No. 1, January 2004, p. 56.

44. Gibbons, David S., *Financing Micro-finance for Poverty Reduction,* Shelter, Human Settlement Management Institute, Vol. VII, No. 1, January 2004, p. 59.

45. Basu, Aparna, *"Women's Empowerment and Self-Help Groups",* Shelter, Human Settlement Management Institute, Vol. VII, No. 1, January 2004, p. 66.

46. Remenyi, Joe, *Micro-finance Best Practice: Ten Parameters of Success for Development NGOs, Shelter,* Human Settlement Management Institute, Vol. VII, No. 1, January 2004, p. 94.

47. Mclaugblin, Delores, *Micro-finance Partnership: Opportunities and Challenges,* Shelter, Human Settlement Management Institute, Vol. VII, No. 1, January 2004, p. 122.

48. Gupta, Shilendra Kumar, *Thrift and Credit Societies (TCS) under SJSRY and Micro-credit, Shelter,* Human Settlement Management Institute, Vol. VII, No. 1, January 2004, p. 124.

49. Sharma, R.H., "Micro-Financing through Self-Help Groups and Non-Government Organisations by Commercial Banks", The *Journal of the Indian Institute of Bankers,* Vol. 70, No. 3, July-September 2002.

50. Lalitha, N., and Nagarajan, *B.S., Self-Help Groups in Rural Development,* Dominant Publishers and Distributors, New Delhi, 2002, I Edition, pp. 8-15.

51. Banerjee, G.D., Financing Agriculture – *In-house Journal of Agricultural Finance Cooperation Ltd.,* Evaluation Study on Self-Help Group, April-June 2002.

52. Surat Singh, "Empowerment of Women Representatives in Panchayat Raj, A Profile from Haryana", *Kurukshetra,* August 2004, pp. 17-20.

53. Singh, Naresh, "Income Generation and Poverty Alleviation Through Micro-Finance: A Comparative Study of Approaches to Micro-Finance Delivery Systems in Bangladesh and India", *Labour and Development,* Vol. 10, No. 1, June 2004.

54. Pal, Mahi, "Social Development of Rural Woman in India", Kurukshetra, July 2004, pp. 40-42.

55. Soundarapandian, M., "Issues in Rural Credit System", *Kurukshetra,* September 2001.

56. Jha, T.N., "Micro-Credit Finance Models in Bangladesh: Lessons for India", *Yojana,* February 2002, pp. 23-30.

57. Amutha, R., "Self-Help Groups for Reaching Poor", *Yojana,* Vol.15, No.4, January 2006, pp. 45-47.

58. Usha Nandhini, S., Padma Rani, S., "Impact of Micro-finance on Rural Women – Micro-Level Study", *Yojana,* Vol. 16, No. 2, July 2006, p. 30.

59. Rajaram Dasgupta, "An Informal Journey through Self-Help Groups", *Indian Journal of Agricultural Economics,* Vol. 56, No. 3, July-September 2001, pp. 370-386.

60. Datta, Samar K. and M. Raman, "Can Heterogeneity and Social Cohesion Coexist in Self-Help Groups: An Evidence from Group Lending in Andhra Pradesh in India", *Indian Journal of Agricultural Economics,* Vol. 56, No. 3, July-September 2001, pp. 387-400.

61. Namboodiri, N.V., R.L. Shiyani, "Potential Role of Self-Help Groups in Rural Financial Deepening", *Indian Journal of Agricultural Economics,* Vol. 56, No. 3, July-September 2001, pp. 401-409.

62. Satish, P., "Some Issues in the Formation of Self-Help Groups", *Indian Journal of Agricultural Economics,* Vol. 56, No. 3, July-September 2001, pp. 410-418.

63. Dadhich, C.L., "Micro-finance – A Panacea for Poverty Alleviation: A Case Study of Oriental Grameen Project in India", *Indian Journal of Agricultural Economics,* Vol. 56, No. 3, July-September 2001, pp. 419-425.

64. Madheswaran and Mita Dharmadhikary, "Empowering Rural Women through Self-Help Groups: Lessons from Maharashtra Rural Credit Project", *Indian Journal of Agricultural Economics,* Vol. 56, No. 3, July-September 2001, pp. 427-443.

65. Nagnur, Shobha, Geeta Channal and Channamma Nanjayyana-math, "Success Stories Microenterprises for Farm Women", Social Welfare, Vol. 52, No. 3, June 2005, pp. 27-30.

66. Das, Sabyasachi, "Self-Help Groups and Micro-Credit Synergic Integration", *Kurukshetra,* Vol. 51, No. 10, August 2003.

67. Dwarakanath, H.D., "Savings and Credit Movement in Andhra Pradesh Participation of Rural Women", *Kurukshetra,* Vol. 51, No. 10, August 2003, pp. 31-37.

68. Dubhashi, Medha, "Micro-Credit and Empowerment of Women", The Cooperator, Vol. 43, No. 4, October 2005, pp. 152-155.

69. Panda, S.K., "Micro-finance in Economic Empowerment of Weaker Sections", *Yojana,* Vol. 47, No. 3, March 2003, pp. 21-25.

70. Gadekar, H.H., "Women Empowerment Through Mahila SHG Industrial Society Ltd.", *The Cooperator,* Vol. 43, No. 3, September 2005.

71. Mishra, Chittaranjan, SHGs in the Unorganised Garment Sector A Case Study of Madurai", *Kurukshetra,* Vol. 53, No. 8, July 2005, pp. 43-46.

72. Kabeer, Naila, "Is Micro-finance a 'Magic Bullet' for Women's Empowerment" Analysis of Findings from South Asia", *Economic and Political Weekly,* Vol. XL, Nos. 45-46, October 29, 2005, pp. 4709-4718.

73. Narayana Reddy, G., "Empowering Women Through Self-Help Groups and Micro-Credit: The Case of NIRD Action Research Projects", *Journal of Rural Development,* Vol. 21(4), October-December 2002, NIRD, Hyderabad, pp. 511-535.

74. Mahajan, Vijay, "From Micro-credit to Livelihood Finance", *Economic and Political Weekly,* Vol. XL, No. 41, October 8, 2005.

Profile of Study Area

INTRODUCTION

Kanyakumari district lies at the southern most tip of peninsular India where Indian Ocean, the Arabian Sea and the Bay of Bengal embrace one another. By its very location, this district occupies a unique place among the districts of Tamil Nadu. One of the most important pilgrim centres of India, Kanyakumari is famous for its tourist attractions.

Enjoying comparatively high rates of rainfall and fertile soils the district is also called ‘Nanjil Nadu’, legendary for agricultural productivity. Kanyakumari has a high literacy rate in the State. One can witness the rare scene of the setting of sun and the rising of moon simultaneously on the full moon day at the cape in Kanyakumari.

LOCATION AND DEMOGRAPHY

The District is situated between 8 8′ – 8 29′ northern latitude and 76 9′ – 77 41′ eastern longitudes, occupying a total area of 1672 sq.km. It is bordered with Thirunelveli district in the North and Northeast, Kerala in the Northwest, Arabian Sea in the West, Indian Ocean in the South, the Gulf of Mannar in the East and Bay of Bengal. It has a coastline of 68 km stretched on the three sides. According to 1991 census, the total population of Kanyakumari district was 16 lakh. The southern tip of the western ghats tapers off into the district and the terrain is a mix of hills, hilly plains and coastal plains.

This small district is famous for its vast green fields, coconut groves, forest wealth and is dotted with a large number of ponds.

History

Kanyakumari has its ancient history dating back to the Sangam age and is a cradle of civilization in this part of India. The district has a large number of historic monuments and temples. Series of kingdoms are known to have ruled Kanyakumari. The most important being the Chera, Chola and Pandya. Up to early fifties of this century, this region was part of Travancore Samasthanam, present day Kerala, where the Tamil speaking majority population struggled to merge with Tamil Nadu and Kanyakumari became part of Tamil Nadu after the constitution of the State Re-organizing Commission in 1956. On the recommendations of the commission, Agasteeswaram, Thovalai, Kalkulam, Vilavancode and Senkottai taluks were given to Tamil Nadu, among which the first four taluks were grouped to form a new Kanyakumari district. On 1st November 1956 the present Kanyakumari district came into existence with headquarters at Nagercoil.

Climate

Kanyakumari district has the unique advantage of rainfall during the southwest and northeast monsoons. The period of southwest monsoon is from June to September while that of northeast monsoon is from October to December. Because of its nearness to the equator, its geography and other climate factors, the growth of various food and non-food crops is favoured. Rainfall is generally high in the northern parts of the district. The annual rainfall ranges between 90 and 160 cm and the average is 140 cm. The general climate of the district is a mild and pleasant for a tropical location. The monsoon winds, the proximity of the sea and the mountains and forests of Western Ghats greatly influence the climate of this district.

Revenue Jurisdiction

The district is divided into two revenue divisions viz., Padmanabhapuram and Nagercoil, having headquarters at Thuckalay and Nagecoil respectively. There are four taluks namely, Vilavancode, Kalkulam, Agasteeswaram and Thovalai and 82 revenue villages. The district has four municipalities Nagercoil, Padmanabhapuram, Colachel and Kuzhithurai.

Development Jurisdiction

This district has been divided into two development divisions namely, Nagercoil and Padmanabhapuram having headquarters at Nagercoil and Thuckalay respectively. The district has been divided into 9 Panchayat Unions namely Agasteeswaram, Thovalai, Rajakkamangalam, Kurunthencode, Thuckalay, Thiruvattar, Killiyoor, Melpuram and Munchirai. Table 3.1 gives the details of development jurisdiction of the district.

Table 3.1. Development Jurisdiction of Kanyakumari District

Sl. No.	Name of the Development Division	Name of the Panchayat Union	Office Location	Area (Sq.km)
1.	Nagercoil	Agasteeswaram	Perumalpuram	143.26
		Rajakkamangalam	Pazhavilai	135.49
		Thovalai	Boothapandy	360.91
		Kurunthencode	Kurunthencode	100.54
		Thuckalay	Kozhiporvilai	127.41
		Thiruvattar	Thiruvattar	88.37
2.	Padmanabha-puram	Killiyoor	Tholayavattam	138.86
		Munchirai	Munchirai	71.45
		Melpuram	Pacode	27.57

Source: Records of District Rural Development Department, Nagercoil.

Based on physiography, the district can be divided into three natural divisions:

1. The north-eastern portion of the Thovalai taluk constitutes a mountainous division with spurs from Western Ghats running into it, called high lands.
2. The west and south-west portion of the district is the sea coast which is flat and fairly fertile and called the low lands.
3. Between the mountain range (high lands) and the seacoast (low lands) there exists a strip of undulating valley the midlands with a few streams available for cultivation.

Land and Irrigation

Over twenty per cent of the total land in Kanyakumari district has moderate limitation for agricultural uses, 74.4 per cent has severe limitations and remaining 5.4 per cent very severe limitation for agricultural uses. Soil in this district is mostly of red loam variety. Laterite type of soil is found in Thiruvattar, Munchirai, Kurunthencode, Rajakkamangalam, Thuckalay and Melpuram Blocks. Mixed type of red loam and laterite with coastal alluvium is found in the western side. The coastal alluvium has high fertility. In terms of soil fertility most of the blocks have low content of Nitrogen, Phosphorus and Potash. The pH value of the soil generally ranges from 4.5 to 8. The district is comparatively well irrigated and the Pechipparai dam and canal network built a century back, one of the oldest dams of erstwhile Travancore, forms the lifeline of the district. Large number of tanks also plays a major role in the predominantly agrarian district.

Land Irrigated by Various Sources

Table 3.2 gives the details of land irrigated by various sources:

Table 3.2. Land Irrigated by Various Sources

Type of Irrigation	Area Irrigated (in Hectares)
Canals	11,114
Tanks	15,794
Wells	1,220
Other sources	468
Total	29,071

Source: Records of District Rural Development Department, Nagercoil.

Agriculture

Rice is the principal food crop in this district. In the hills, plantation crops such as tea, coffee, rubber and pepper are being raised. In the lower slopes of the hills, tapioca and banana are raised as rain-fed crops. In the plains paddy, tapioca, coconut and vegetables are raised as main crops. Paddy, tapioca, coconut and rubber are the main crops in this district. Kanyakumari district is the only one in Tamil Nadu where rubber is grown on a large scale.

(*i*) Total cultivated area in hectares 1,00,653.

(*ii*) Net area sown in hectares 82,680.

(*iii*) Area sown more than once in hectares 17,973.

Population

According to 1991 census, the total population of Kanyakumari district was 16,00,340. The male population is 8,03,989 and the female population is 7,06,510. In this district the rural population is more than the urban population. The rural population is 13,30,240 and the urban population is 8,70,100. The density of population is high with 957 per sq.km. The total literates in this district are 11,48,778.

The population and the literacy rates of Blocks and Municipalities were shown in the Table 3.3.

Table 3.3. The Population, Sex Ratio and Literacy Rates of the Blocks and Municipalities of Kanyakumari District 2000-2001

Name of the Block/ Municipalities	Area (Sq.km)	Population			Literate		
		Persons	Male	Female	Persons	Male	Female
Agasteeswaram	143.26	132413	65460	66953	97756	50218	47538
Rajakkamangalam	135.49	127325	63980	63345	92573	48516	44057
Thovalai	360.91	97802	49117	48685	71075	37722	33353
Kurunthencode	109.54	97802	49117	48685	71075	37722	33353
Thuckalay	127.41	162019	81739	80280	117437	61607	55830
Thiruvattar	88.37	159182	80261	78921	109262	57402	51860
Killiyoor	138.86	151.34	76515	74519	105231	55695	49536
Munchirai	71.45	175454	88584	86870	116533	61656	54877
Melpuram	277.57	173426	86422	87004	120296	63380	56916
Nagercoil Municipality	19.37	190084	94834	95250	152274	78393	73881
Padmanabhapuram	6.47	19269	6980	9589	14961	7875	7086
Colachel	5.18	24305	12320	11985	16822	8731	8091
Kuzhithurai	5.15	19226	9467	9759	14740	7513	7227

Source: Records of the District Rural Development Department, Nagercoil.

Forests

The forests are highly enchanting with pleasant sholas, beautiful grass lands, panoramic valleys, top hillocks, singing streams, vast stretches of rubber plantations, valuable teak plantations and an immense treasure of medicinal plants. The Government reserve forests occupy an area of 50486 hectares. They cover 30.2 per cent of the geographical area in Kanyakumari district. The yield per hectare of forest is probably the highest in Tamil Nadu with an yield of 200 to 275 cubic metres.[1]

Table 3.4 shows the total forest area in Kanyakumari district.

Table 3.4. Forest Area in Kanyakumari District

(In hectares)

Year	Forest Area
1990	54155
1991	49369
1992	49369
1993	49369
1994	54211
1995	49369
1996	49354
1997	54155
1998	54155
1999	54155
2000	54155

Source: Records of District Forest Office, Nagercoil.

These forests supply timber and firewood. People collect firewood from these forests illegally. Government timber and firewood usually come under the hammer.

Revenue of the Forest Department of Kanyakumari District

Table 3.5 shows the revenue obtained annually from the sale of timber and firewood.

Rubber Trees

The northern part of the district, which is at the foot of the Western Ghats is highly suitable for the cultivation of rubber. Hence the state has been taking special efforts to expand the area under this crop. These rubber plantations produce not only latex but also wood logs and twigs as well. The rubber trees are cut down after 15 to 20 years of plantation. Table

3.6 shows the area under rubber trees over the years. These wood log and twigs are used by the households as non-commercial energy sources.

Table 3.5. Revenue of the Forest Department of Kanyakumari District

Year	Timber and Firewood	Minor Forest Produce (in Rs.)
1991-92	962713.00	2130002.00
1992-93	2687725.00	211261.00
1993-94	3654030.00	22166.00
1994-95	4632511.00	190815.00
1995-96	2477025.00	236587.00
1996-97	1649622.00	516450.00

Source: Records of Forest Department, Nagercoil.

Table 3.6. Area under Rubber Trees

Year	Area (in hectare)	Year	Area (in hectare)
1989-90	15699	1995-96	22089
1990-91	15781	1996-97	19478
1991-92	21249	1997-98	18063
1992-93	21198	1998-99	18068
1993-94	21406	1999-2000	18450
1994-95	21663		

Sources: 1. District Statistical Hand Book – Kanyakumari District.
2. Horticulture Office, Nagercoil.

Coconut Trees

Coconut is a major plantation crop, cultivated extensively in this district. The climatic condition of this district is quite conducive for coconut cultivation. The stalk and spadix obtained from coconut trees are very good non-commercial energy sources for households. Most of the households have been using these sources of energy traditionally for cooking and heating purposes. Table 3.7 shows the area under coconut trees over the years.

Table 3.7. Area under Coconut Trees

(In hectares)

Year	Forest Area
1989-90	25100
1990-91	23230
1991-92	18408
1992-93	18717
1993-94	19177
1994-95	19241
1995-96	20719
1996-97	21100
1997-98	21197
1998-99	21517
1999-2000	21670

Tapioca

Tapioca is the major tuber crop grown in this district. The climate and soil conditions are quite suitable for the cultivation of this crop. The tapioca stems and leaves are used for fuel purposes in rural households. Table 3.8 shows the area under tapioca cultivation over the years.

Table 3.8. Area under Tapioca

(In hectares)

Year	Forest Area
1989-90	10400
1990-91	10030
1991-92	9337
1992-93	9683
1993-94	9598
1994-95	9514
1995-96	9255
1996-97	8297
1997-98	9715
1998-99	9453
1999-2000	8568
2000-2001	8678

Source: 1. District Statistical Hand Book – Kanyakumari District.
2. Horticulture Office, Nagercoil.

Area of Trees and Groves

Apart from forest, this district is covered by vegetations of every type with the passage of time they will also move to be a very good source of fuel wood. Table 3.9 shows the area in hectares in Kanyakumari district.

Plantation in Kanyakumari District

Plantations raised in Kanyakumari district by forest department is shown in Table 3.10.

Table 3.9. Area under Miscellaneous Trees and Groves in Kanyakumari District

(In hectares)

Year	Area
1990	359
1991	475
1992	420
1993	410
1994	217
1995	515
1996	473
1997	420
1998	418

Source: 1. District Statistical Hand Book – Kanyakumari District.
2. Horticulture Office, Nagercoil.

Table 3.10. Plantations Raised in Kanyakumari District by Forest Department

Name of the Plants	Area (in Hectares)
Teak	2271.00
Softwood	2537.00
Bamboos	102.00
Eucalyptus	37.00
Tamarind	75.0
Total	5022.00

Source: Records of District Forest Office, Nagercoil.

The timber obtained from these sources depend 128 saw mills and 115 timber depots. Further, as much as 150 tonnes of timber is smuggled out of the forests and plantations.

Electricity

Kanyakumari district has one hydroelectric project, which is located at Kodayar. The installed capacity of this power plant is 6 MW and 4 MW. This project has two plants. The power generated by these two hydroelectric plants is given in the Table 3.11.

Table 3.11. Power Generation in Power House I and II

(In Hectares)

Year	Area
1990	174.170
1991	280.426
1992	272.465
1993	334.554
1994	167.789
1995	322.243
1996	322.700
1997	169.137
1998	213.623
1999	228.669

Source: TNEB Kodayar Power House.

Power Generation of TNEB and Private Wind Mills

Power generation by windmills is gathering momentum in Tamil Nadu. The windmills in Muppandal have won national acclaim for their enormous power generation potentials. What is unique about the wind speed in Muppandal is that, it is the highest in the whole of Asia. In this area both the Tamil Nadu Electricity Board and private concerns have installed windmills. The Tamil Nadu Electricity Board owns 20 windmills and the remaining mills are owned by private parties. The total generation of the Tamil Nadu Electricity

Board and private windmills in the study area is shown in Table 3.12.

Table 3.12. Power Generation by TNEB and the Private Wind Mills

Year	Total Number of Wind Mills	Area
1990	26	11580236
1991	28	12443296
1992	35	17178657
1993	110	38016217
1994	324	84186609
1995	369	109980759
1996	423	161221398
1997	445	147800428
1998	457	174311930
1999	463	211077662

Source: TNEB, Muppandal.

Domestic Electricity Services of Kanyakumari District

There are five sub-stations namely Nagercoil with a storage capacity of 110/33-11 KV and 110/11 KV, Thuckalay 110/11/ KV, Pechipparai 110/11/KV, Kuzhithurai 110/KV and Kottaram 33/11KV. The major power consumers are the households and the industrial sector.[1]

Industries

The important industries located in the district are:

(*a*) Indian Rare Earths Limited,

(*b*) Kanyaspin Limited,

(*c*) Nagammal Mills Limited,

(*d*) TAC Floor Company.

Among the small scale industries, those which deserve a special mention would include the cashew industry, the match industry, the wooden furniture industry, the oil industry, the brick industry and the printing industry. In the cottage industries sector the palm leaf industry, the fibre industry, the bee keeping industry, the beedi industry, the handloom industry have assumed very great prominence over the years. Further, crafts like the lace making, sculpture, wood carving and shell works are tending to fade into oblivion with the passage of time.

Economic Background of the District

Agriculture is the chief occupation of the people in this district. Paddy, tapioca, coconut, banana, rubber, cashew, mango, pineapple and groundnut are the important crops raised. Excepting paddy, all the other crops are raised under rainfed conditions. Tapioca is a subsidiary food for the middle class and the working class and it is cultivated in 1065 hectares.[2]

Crops such as tea, coffee, rubber, coconut, cocoa, pineapple and pepper are cultivated in the high lands. Coconut, arecanut, paddy, banana, groundnut and vegetables are cultivated in the middle lands. Mango, citrus, and jack are important fruit trees raised in orchards. Coconut groves are concentrated in Agasteeswaram, Rajakkamangalam, Thiruvattar, Munchirai, Killiyoor, and Kurunthencode. Rubber is cultivated in about 128000 hectares mostly in Kalkulam and Vilavancode taluks.[3]

Roads

The district has a good network of roads connecting the important villages and towns in the district. Important commercial centres like Vadasery, Kottar, Manavalakurichi, Kaliakkailai, Marthandam, Puthukadai and Karungal are connected by roads with other districts in Tamil Nadu and the States of Karnataka and Kerala. The total length of roads in the district is 1863 kms. They cover 62.4 km of National Highways, 48 km of State Highways, 975 km maintained by Municipalities, district authorities and public works department. The remaining roads are maintained by panchayats and panchayt unions. The length of the roads in the district per 100 sq.km. of area is 110 km as against the state average of 30 km.[5]

Railways

This district is linked with places throughout the country by means of railways. The distance of the railway line from Nagercoil to Trivandrum is 66 km. From Nagercoil to Tirunelveli junction is 77 km and from Nagercoil to Cape Comorin is 15.51 kms. The length of broad gauge railway line in the district is about 70.41 km. The important railway stations are Kuzhithurai, Eraniel, Palliyadi, Nagercoil, Thovalai, Suchindrum, Agasteeswaram and Cape Comorin.[6]

SUMMARY

The long and short of what has been said so far about the study area is that it has been endowed variously and copiously with enormous reserve of environmental resources which can maintain a steady supply of every type of non-commercial energy sources for years on end.

REFERENCES

1. Kanyakumari District Forest Division, Tamil Nadu Forest Department.
2. Kanyakumari District, *The Hindecon*, Vol. I, 1992, p. 30.
3. Credit Plan for Kanyakumari District, Tamil Nadu, Indian Overseas Bank, Madras, 1988-90, p. 4.
4. Credit Plan for Kanyakumari District, Tamil Nadu, Indian Overseas Bank, Madras, 1988-90, p. 4.
5. *Ibid.*, pp. 43-44.
6. Kanyakumari District, *The Hindecon,* Vol. I, 1992, p. 30.

Micro-finance and Self-help Groups - Performance Analysis

The present chapter has been divided into two parts. The first part explains the emergence of micro-finance in India and the performance of micro-finance activities under SGSY scheme. The Self-help Groups' linkage with the micro-finance performance is analysed in the second part of the chapter.

MICRO-FINANCE AND SELF-HELP GROUPS

Micro-finance

Micro-finance refers to small savings, credit and insurance services extended to socially and economically disadvantaged segments of the society. In the Indian context terms such as "small and marginal farmers", "rural artisans" and "economically weaker sections" have been used to broadly define micro-finance customers. The recent Task Force on micro-finance has defined it as "Provision of thrift, credit and other financial services and products of very small amounts to the poor in rural, semi-urban areas, for enabling them to raise their income levels and improve living standards". At present, a large part of micro-finance activity is confined to credit only. Women constitute a vast majority of users of micro-credit and savings services.

Demand of Micro-Finance Services in India

Due to its large size and population of around 1000 million, India's GDP ranks among the top 15 economies of the world.

However, around 300 million people or about 60 million households are living below the poverty line. It is further estimated that of these households, only about 20 per cent have access to credit from the formal sector. Additionally, the segment of the rural population above the poverty line but not rich enough to be of interest to the formal financial institutions, also does not have good access to the formal financial intermediary services, including savings services.

A group of micro-finance practitioners estimated the annualised credit usage of all poor families (rural and urban) at over Rs.45,000 crore, of which some 80 per cent is met by informal sources. This figure has been extrapolated using the numbers of rural and urban poor households and their average annual credit usage (Rs. 6,000 and Rs. 9,000 pa respectively) assessed through various micro studies.

Credit on reasonable terms to the poor can bring about a significant reduction in poverty. It is with this hypothesis, micro-credit assumes significance in the Indian context. With about 60 million households below or just above the austerely defined poverty line and with more than 80 per cent unable to access credit at reasonable rates, it is obvious that there are certain issues and problems, which have prevented the reach of micro-finance to the needy.

With globalization and liberalization of the economy, opportunities for the unskilled and the illiterate are not increasing fast enough, as compared to the rest of the economy. This is leading to a lopsided growth in the economy thus increasing the gap between the haves and have-nots. It is in this context, the institutions involved in micro-finance have a significant role to play to reduce this disparity and lead to more equitable growth.

In terms of demand for micro-credit, there are three segments:

(*i*) At the very bottom in terms of income and assets, and most numerous, are those who are landless and are engaged in agricultural work on a seasonal basis and manual labourers in forestry, mining, household industries, construction and transport. This segment requires, first and foremost, consumption credit during those months when they do not get labour work, and for contingencies such as illness. They also need credit for acquiring small productive assets, such as livestock, using which they can generate additional income.

(*ii*) The next market segment is small and marginal farmers and rural artisans, weavers and those self-employed in the urban informal sector as hawkers, vendors, and workers in household micro-enterprises. This segment mainly needs credit for working capital, a small part of which also serves consumption needs. In rural areas, one of the main uses of working capital is for crop production. This segment also needs term credit for acquiring additional productive assets, such as irrigation pumpsets, borewells and livestock in case of farmers and equipment (looms, machinery) and worksheds in case of non-farm workers. This market segment also largely comprises the poor but not the poorest.

(*iii*) The third market segment is of small and medium farmers who have gone in for commercial crops such as surplus paddy and wheat, cotton, groundnut, and others engaged in dairying, poultry, fishery, etc. Among non-farm activities, this segment includes those in villages and slums, engaged in processing or manufacturing activity, running provision stores, repair workshops, tea shops and various services enterprises. These persons are not always poor, though they live barely above the poverty line and also suffer from inadequate access to formal credit.

One market segment, which is of great importance to micro-credit is women. The 1991 Census figures reveal that out of a total 2.81 million marginal workers, 2.54 million were women and their further break-up shows that out of a total of 2.67 million rural marginal workers, 2.44 million were females. Further, many more women were willing to work. This has been explained by the results of a survey done by the National Sample Survey Organization (NSSO), 43rd round, which has revealed that there is a wide variety of work which rural women combine with household work.

In the NSSO survey it has also been estimated that a large percentage of rural women in the age group of 15 years and above, who are usually engaged in household work, are willing to accept work at household premises (29.3%), in activities such as dairy (9.5%), poultry (3%), cattle rearing, spinning and weaving (3.4%), tailoring (6.1%) and manufacturing of wood and cane products etc. Amongst the women surveyed, 27.5 per cent rural women were seeking regular full-time work and 65.3 per cent were seeking part-time work. To start or to carry on such work, 53.6 per cent women wanted initial finance on easy terms, and 22.2 per cent wanted working capital facilities.

Supply of Micro-Finance Services

RBI data shows that informal sources provide a significant part of the total credit needs of the rural population. The magnitude of the dependence of the rural poor on informal sources of credit can be observed from the findings of the All India Debt and Investment Survey, 1992, which shows that the share of the non-institutional agencies (informal sector) in the outstanding cash dues of the rural households was 36 per cent. However, the dependence of rural households on such informal sources had reduced their total outstanding dues steadily from 83.7 per cent in 1961 to 36 per cent in 1991.

Among formal institutional sources, banks and co-operatives provided credit support to almost 56 per cent of the rural households, while professional and agricultural money lenders were providing credit to almost one sixth of the rural households.

Though the overall share of institutional credit for rural households has gone up steadily, households in the lower asset groups were more dependent on the non-institutional credit agencies. The share of debt from the non-institutional credit agencies was 58 per cent in the case of lowest asset group of 'less than Rs.5000' as against a low of 19 per cent in the highest asset group of "Rs.2.5 lakh and above".

Over the decades following India's independence in 1947, Government of India (GOI) has made concerted efforts to provide micro-finance to the rural poor through the formal financial sector namely the co-operatives. However, the limited success of the co-operatives in the mid fifties to the sixties forged the need for nationalization of commercial banks (CB) in 1971 and the establishment of a large network to reach every village, and every segment of the population. In the mid-1970s, Regional Rural Banks (RRB) were also established to continue further the outreach of the banking sector in reaching the rural poor. All these programmes were supported by a policy of mandated credit programmes for the low-income households that were supported by the Integrated Rural Development Programme (IRDP), launched in 1980. The IRDP was designed to provide a mix of subsidy from the government and credit from the banking system to enable the asset acquisition of the poor.

As a result of these programmes, India has one of the largest banking networks in the world with close to 50,000 CB outlets; 14,420 RRBs; and 90,000 primary agricultural co-operative societies. Close to 43 percent of the CB, and RRB branches are located in the rural areas. Even more impressive is the fact that there is a financial intermediary branch for every 15,000 households, and a co-operative in every village.

Due to the extensive expansion of the banking network and emphasis on lending to small borrowers, there have been a lot of small loans by banks. In terms of amount, this was 13.2 per cent of the total credit outstanding from commercial banks and RRBs. As per RBI data for March 1994, the number of accounts below Rs.25,000 was 5.6 million, or 93.6 per cent of total loan accounts, with 18.6 per cent of the outstanding amount. Of these, accounts with outstanding below Rs. 75,000 comprised 80.5 per cent of the number of accounts and 49.5 per cent of amount outstanding. In terms of purpose, 45.8 per cent of amount was for small agricultural loans, 20.2 per cent for industry and 18.8 per cent for trade and services.

By March 1997, the number of small borrower's accounts with a credit limit below Rs.25,000 had come down by as many 0.6 million accounts to 5 million, or 90.1 per cent of the outstanding loan accounts. This decline in number of accounts clearly shows the post liberalization trend, with banks concentrating their efforts on larger loans and becoming even more reluctant to extend credit to small borrowers.

While banks have been engaged in financing small borrowers, the manner in which this is being done can hardly be called micro-finance. The procedures are cumbersome, the staff unfriendly and the transaction costs high. Repeated loans, except for crop production, are rare, even for borrowers who have repaid fully. Furthermore, even though many of the loans extended to the poor by the public sector financial institutions are subsidized, their ultimate cost to the borrowers is high factoring in out-of-pocket costs, payments to middle men, wage and business loss due to time spent in getting the loan approved. Effectively, the total cost of funds to the borrower ranges between 22-30 per cent as against the 12-14 per cent nominal lending rates specified for commercial bank loans below Rs.2,00,000. All this results in low repayment rates, leading to a vicious cycle of non-availability and non-repayment.

SWARNAJEYANTHI GRAM SWAROZGAR YOJANA (SGSY)

Swarnajeyanthi Gram Swarozgar Yojana is the single largest self-employment programme for the rural poor launched from April 1999. A significant aspect of SGSY is that every family assisted under this programme is to be brought above the poverty line over a period of three years and therefore the programme aims at creating substantial additional incomes for the rural poor.

The SGSY will be funded by the Centre and the State in the ratio of 75:25.

Swarnajeyanthi Gram Swarzgoar Yojana aims at establishing a large number of micro-enterprises in the rural areas, building upon the potential of the rural poor. The assisted families may be individuals or groups emphasis will be on the group approach.

The SGSY also focuses on the group approach. This involves organization of the poor into Self-Help Groups. SGSY has specially focus on the vulnerable groups among the rural poor. Accordingly SC/STs would account for at least 50 per cent, women 40 per cent and the disabled, 3 per cent.

Funds Available Under SGSY in India

The funds available for the SGSY scheme is explained in Table 4.1.

From the Table 4.1, it is clear that during the period of 6 years (1999-2000 to 2004-2005), the total funds allocated for the SGSY programme was Rs. 8,341.36 crore. The trend of the funds allocation shows that there is a declining trend from Rs.1961.97 crore in 1999-2000 to 1061.22 crore in 2004-2005. Both the contribution of Central and State Governments had declined over the period of time. The Central Government released the funds of Rs.869.55 crore in 1999-2000 and it declined to 446.05 crore in 2004-2005. Similarly the State released the total of Rs.261.47 crore in 1999-2000 and Rs.183.82 crore in 2004-2005. The average release of the funds to the Central allocation by Central Government for the SGSY scheme was 65.85 per cent and the State releases to the allocation was 69.86 per cent.

Graphical representation of funds available under SGSY in India is given in Fig. 4.1.

Funds Utilization Under SGSY in India

The funds utilization under SGSY scheme is presented in Table 4.2 and Fig. 4.2.

Table 4.1. Funds Available Under SGSY in India

(Rs. in Crore)

Sl. No.	Items	1999-2000	2000-2001	2001-2002	2002-2003	2003-2004	2004-2005	Total / Average
1.	Total Allocation	1472.33	1332.50	774.50	756.37	1065.83	1332.67	6734.20
2.	Central Allocation	1105.00	1000.00	581.50	567.90	800.00	1000.00	5054.40
3.	State Allocation	367.34	332.50	193.00	188.47	265.83	332.67	1679.81
4.	Central Releases	869.55	462.11	401.10	504.56	645.12	446.05	3328.49
	Percentage of Central Releases	78.69	46.21	68.98	88.85	80.64	44.61	65.85
5.	State Releases	261.47	200.76	156.07	181.14	190.32	183.82	1173.58
	Percentage of State Releases	71.18	60.38	80.87	96.11	71.59	55.26	69.86
6.	Opening Balance as on 1st April	776.62	854.74	661.58	415.77	295.24	352.81	561.15
7.	Misc. Report	54.33	90.57	80.80	76.66	101.63	8.54	80.42
	Total Funds Available	1961.97	1608.18	1299.55	1178.13	1232.31	1061.22	8341.36

Source: Ministry of Rural Development, New Delhi, 2006.

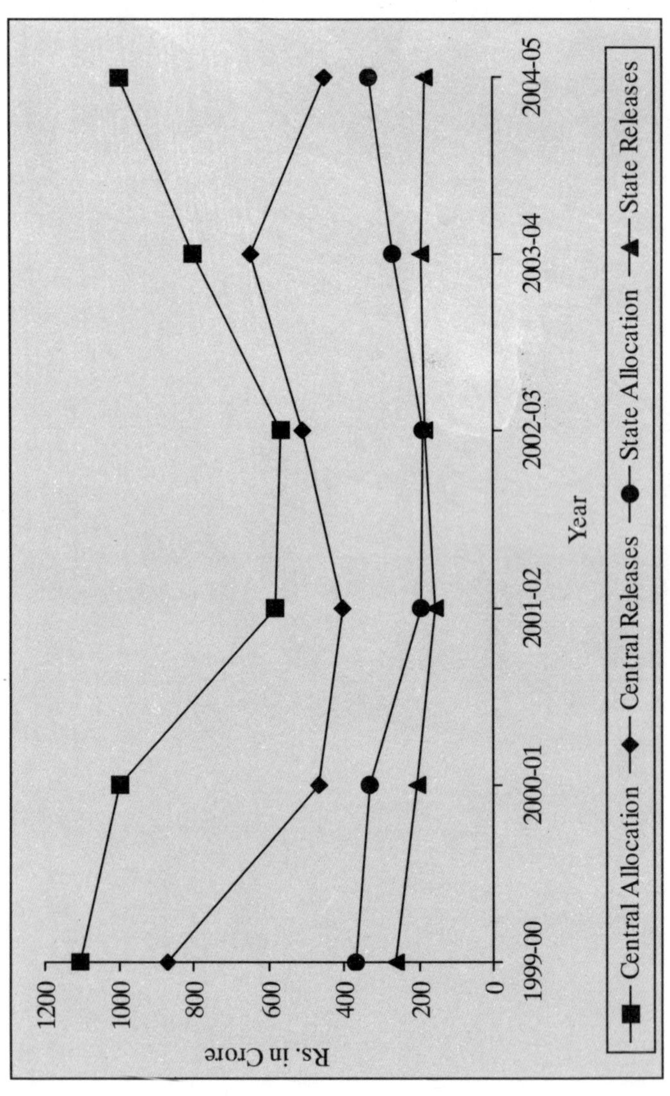

Fig. 4.1. Funds Available Under SGSY in India

Table 4.2. Funds Utilization Under SGSY in India

(Rs. in Crore)

Sl. No.	Items	1999-2000	2000-2001	2001-2002	2002-2003	2003-2004	2004-2005	Total / Average
1.	Total Funds Utilised (Rs.)	959.86	1117.94	970.32	921.11	1065.80	861.92	5896.95
2.	Percentage of Utilisation to Funds Available	48.92	69.52	74.67	78.18	86.49	81.22	73.17
3.	Percentage of Utilisation to Allocation	65.19	83.90	125.28	121.78	100.00	64.68	93.47
4.	Percentage of Utilisation on Subsidy	36.79	52.67	86.16	80.10	65.49	74.42	65.94
5.	Percentage of Utilisation on Infrastructure Dev.	14.45	20.51	19.79	18.01	13.81	16.31	17.15
6.	Percentage of Utilisation on Training / Skill Dev.	3.03	3.62	6.23	5.44	4.67	3.01	4.33

Source : Ministry of Rural Development, New Delhi, 2006.

Table 4.2 reveals that the total funds utilized during the study period of 6 years was Rs.5,896.95 crore. The growth of funds utilization had declined from Rs.959.86 crore in 1999-2000 to Rs.861.92 crore in 2004-05. Only in the year 2000-01, the highest level of funds (Rs.1117.94 crore) were utilized for the SGSY scheme at national level. On the whole the percentage of utilization of funds available for the programme was 73.17 per cent during the 6 year period. The percentage of utilization to funds available was higher (86.49%) in the year 2003-2004. The percentage of utilization to allocation was 93.47 per cent, at an average for the 6 year period. During the year 2001-2002, the per cent of utilization to allocation was 125.28 per cent which shows the best result of funds utilization in India under SGSY scheme.

At an average for the six years of study period, the percentage of utilization on subsidy was 65.94 and the percentage of utilization on infrastructure development was only 17.15 per cent. Similarly, the percentage of utilization on training/skill development was only 4.33 per cent. Both the percentage of funds utilization on infrastructure development and skill training development was very poor in the case of performance of SGSY in India for the past 6 year period.

Performance of Credit Under SGSY in India

The performance of credit under SGSY at national level is exhibited in Table 4.3 and Fig. 4.3.

Table 4.3 reveals that the total credit target under SGSY scheme was Rs.16,773.08 crore during the study period from 1999-2000 to 2004-2005. But the credit mobilized under the SGSY scheme was only Rs.7757.73 crore during the same period and the percentage of credit utilized was 47.46 per cent. The growth of credit mobilization had shown the increasing trend from Rs.1,056.46 crore in 1999-2000 to

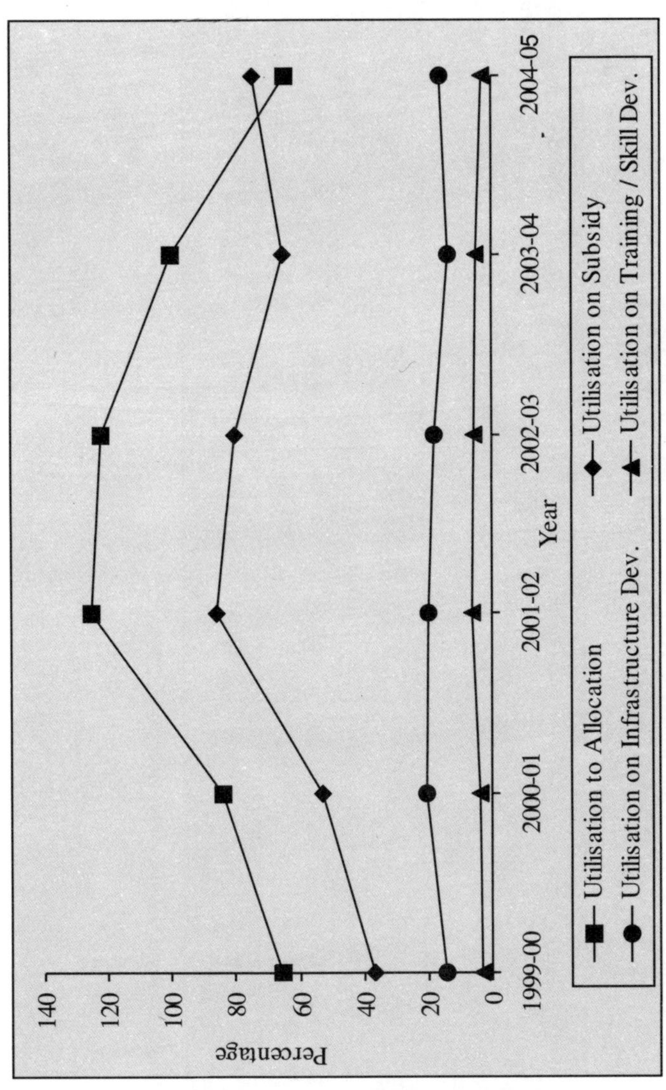

Fig. 4.2. Funds Utilization Under SGSY in India

Table 4.3. Performance of Credit Under SGSY in India

(Rs. in Crore)

Sl. No.	Items	1999-2000	2000-2001	2001-2002	2002-2003	2003-2004	2004-2005	Total / Average
1.	Total Credit Target (Rs.)	3205.00	3205.00	3200.87	2525.21	2129.33	2507.67	16773.08
2.	Total Credit Mobilised (Rs.)	1056.46	1459.44	1329.68	1184.30	1275.24	1452.61	7757.73
3.	Percentage of Credit Mobilized	32.96	45.54	41.54	46.90	59.89	57.93	47.46
4.	Credit Disbursed to SHGs (Rs.)	187.30	256.64	318.34	459.08	763.85	311.28	2296.49

Source : Ministry of Rural Development, New Delhi, 2006.

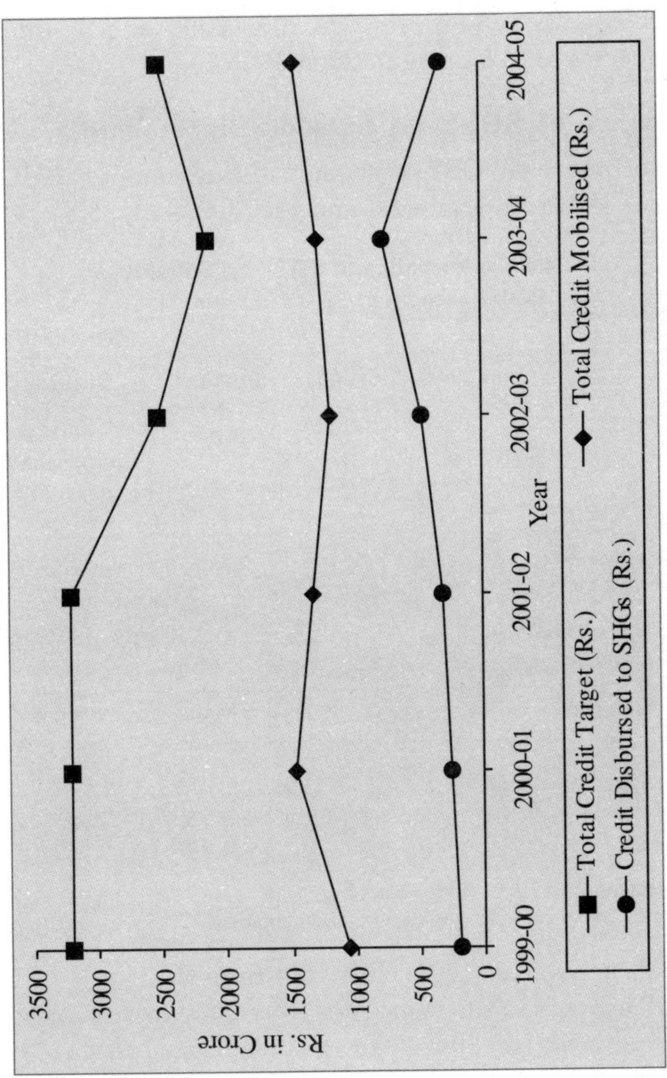

Fig. 4.3. Performance of Credit Under SGSY in India

Rs. 1,452.61 crore in 2004-2005. But the total credit disbursement of SHGs was Rs. 2,296.49 crore. The credit disbursement to SHGs has been increased from Rs.187.30 crore in 1999-2000 to Rs.763.85 crore in 2003-2004 and again it declined to Rs.311.28 crore in 2004-2005.

Performance of SGSY on Subsidy Disbursement

The performance of SGSY on subsidy disbursement to SHGs in India is shown in Table 4.4 and Fig. 4.4.

Table 4.4. Performance of SGSY on Subsidy Disbursement to SHGs in India

(Rs. in Crore)

Sl. No.	Year	Total Subsidy Disbursed	Subsidy Disbursed to SHGs	Subsidy Disbursed to Individual Swarozgaries
1.	1999-2000	541.69	124.58	417.11
2.	2000-2001	701.85	167.93	533.92
3.	2001-2002	665.62	209.94	455.68
4.	2002-2003	605.89	282.53	323.36
5.	2003-2004	697.97	472.64	225.33
6.	2004-2005	641.41	250.81	390.60
	Total	3854.43 (99.99)	1508.43 (39.13)	2346.00 (60.87)

Source: Ministry of Rural Development, New Delhi, 2006.
Note: Figures within parentheses denotes percentages.

From the Table 4.4, it is clear that from the inception of the SGSY scheme to the year from 1999-2000 to 2004-2005, the total subsidy disbursed to the beneficiaries was Rs. 3,854.43 crore. Of the total subsidy, disbursed, 1,508.43 crore (39.13%) were only disbursed to the Self-Help Groups under SGSY. Only Rs. 2,346 crore (60.87%) were disbursed to the

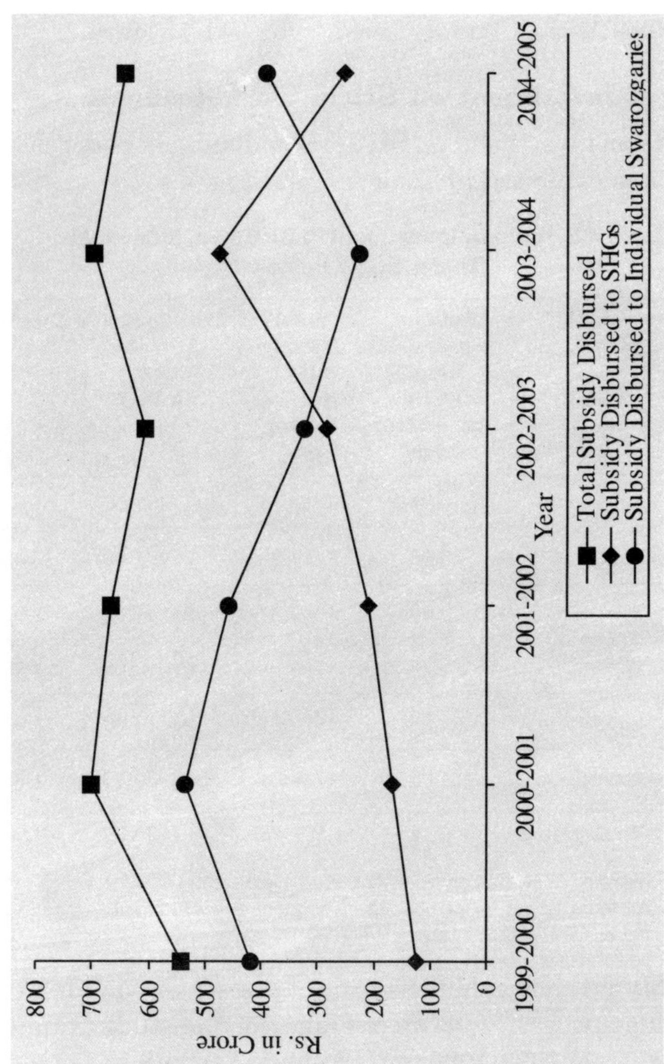

Fig. 4.4. Performance of SGSY on Subsidy Disbursement to SHGs in India

individual swarozgaries of SGSY. The growth of total subsidy distribution had increased gradually from Rs.541.69 crore in 1999-2000 to Rs.697.97 crore in 2003-2004. But in the year 2004-2005, it had declined to Rs.641.41 crore.

Ratio of Investment on SHGs Vs. Individuals

The ratio of investment on SHGs vs. individuals under SGSY in India is exhibited in Table 4.5 and Fig. 4.5.

Table 4.5. Ratio of Investment in SHGs Vs. Individuals Under SGSY in India

Sl. No.	Year	Ratio of Investment on SHGs vs. Individuals	Total Investment (Rs. in Crore)	Per Capital Investment (in Rs.)	Credit Subsidy Ratio
1.	1999-2000	0.24	1598.15	17113.00	1.95
2.	2000-2001	0.24	2161.29	21481.00	2.08
3.	2001-2002	0.36	1995.30	21284.00	2.00
4.	2002-2003	0.71	1790.18	21666.00	1.95
5.	2003-2004	1.68	1973.22	22533.00	1.83
6.	2004-2005	1.08	1714.01	24958.00	1.85
	Total/Average	0.72	11,232.15	21505.83	1.94

Source: Ministry of Rural Development, New Delhi, 2006.
Note: All India target for per capita investment and credit subsidy ratio are Rs.25,000 and 3:1 respectively.

Table 4.5 shows that the ratio of investment on SHGs Vs individuals was 0.72, at an average, for the study period of six years from 1999-2000 to 2004-2005. The total investment under SGSY was increased from Rs.1,598.15 crore in 1999-2000 to Rs.1,714.01 crore in 2004-2005. The total investment of the SGSY scheme was Rs.11,232.15 crore during the study

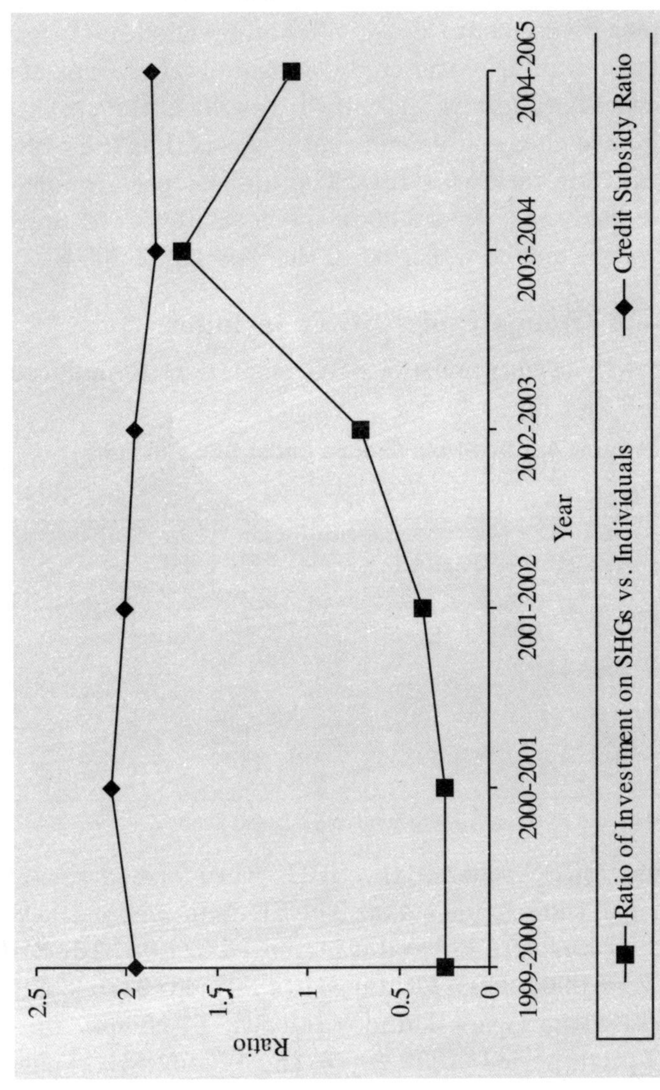

Fig. 4.5. Ratio of Investment in SHGs Vs. Individuals Under SGSY in India

period. The All India target for per capita investment is Rs.25,000. But the average per capita investment was Rs.21,505.83 during the six year period. In 2004-2005, the per capita investment (Rs.24,958) had reached the target of Rs.25,000. Similarly, the credit subsidy ratio target of the Government of India is 3:1. But the results of the past years performance on credit subsidy ratio shows that the average credit subsidy ratio was 1.94. The highest performance on credit subsidy ratio was 2.08 in the year 2000-2001 and the lowest performance was 1.83 in the year 2003-2004.

Self-Help Groups Under SGSY in India

The growth performance of SHG formation is analysed in Table 4.6 and Fig. 4.6.

Table 4.6. Self-Help Groups under SGSY in India

(In Nos.)

Sl. No.	Items	1999-2000	2000-2001	2001-2002	2002-2003	2003-2004	2004-2005	Total/ Average
1.	Self-Help Groups formed since 01.04.1999	292426	515691	950078	1343914	1950599	1987167	7039875
2.	Number of SHGs passed Grade-I	125402	214011	176002	189634	203624	233633	1142306
3.	Number of SHGs passed Grade-II	74234	101291	54040	96020	91405	98291	515281

Source: Ministry of Rural Development, New Delhi, 2006.

Under SGSY scheme, the SHGs were formed since the inception of the scheme 1.4.99. The SHGs formed in the year 1999-2000 was 2,92,426 and it increased to 1,987,167 SHGs in the year 2004-2005. Of the SHGs formed, 233633 SHGs had passed the Grade-I under the SGSY scheme. During the inception period (1999-2000), the 125402 SHGs passed the Grade-II of the SGSY scheme. The passing of Grade-I and Grade-II by the SHGs was 233633 and 98291 respectively in the year 2004-2005.

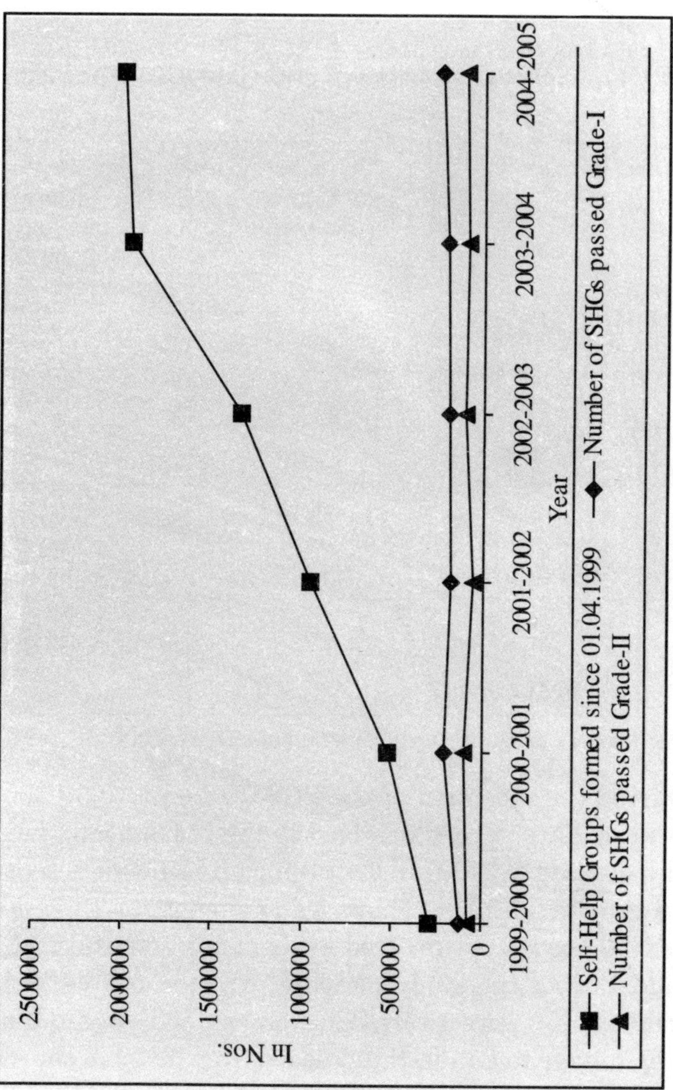

Fig. 4.6. Self-Help Groups Under SGSY in India

Economic Activities of SHGs

The SHGs involved in the economic activities is presented in Table 4.7 and Fig. 4.7.

Table 4.7. Economic Activities of SHGs Under SGSY in India

(In Nos.)

Sl. No.	Year	SHGs taking up Economic Activities	Percentage of SHGs taking up Economic Activity to Grade-II
1.	1999-2000	29017	39.09
2.	2000-2001	26317	25.98
3.	2001-2002	30576	56.58
4.	2002-2003	35317	36.78
5.	2003-2004	50242	54.97
6.	2004-2005	51291	52.18
	Total/Average	222760	44.26

Source: Ministry of Rural Development, New Delhi, 2006.

During the inception of the SGSY scheme (1999-2000), there were 29017 SHGs involved in the economic activities and it increased to 51291 SHGs taking up economic activities in the year 2004-2005. There was tremendous growth in the case of the SHGs involved in economic activities. At an average, during the study period of 6 years, the 44.26 per cent of the SHGs were involved in economic activities in India. The percentage to Grade-II increased from 39.09 in the year 1999-2000 to 52.18 in 2004-2005.

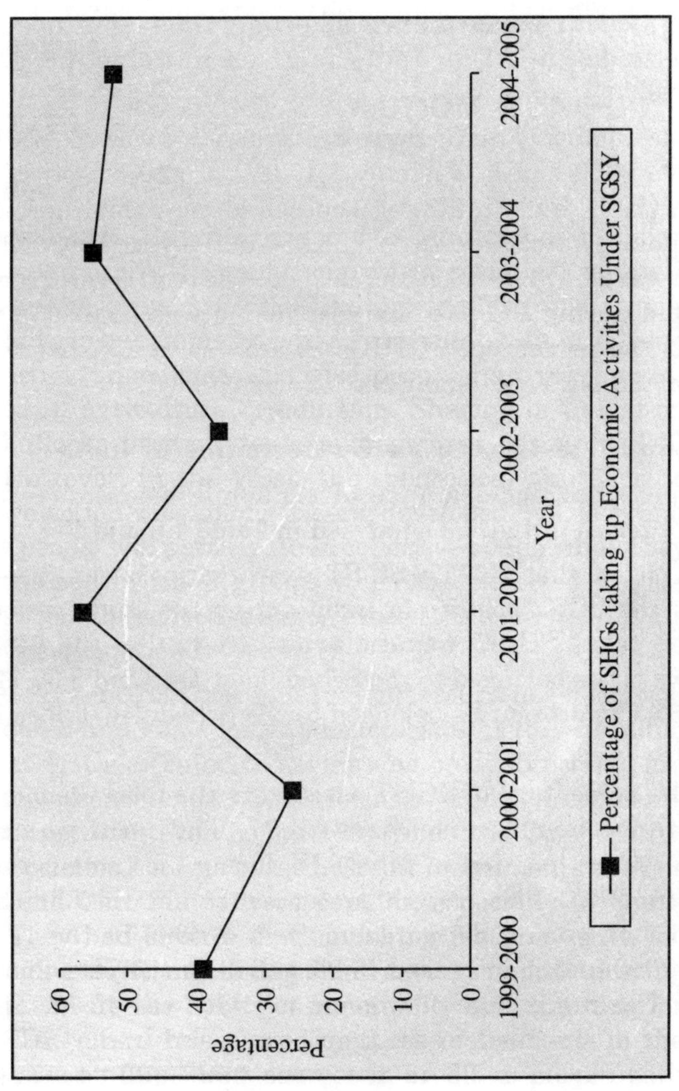

Fig. 4.7. Economic Activities of SHGs Under SGSY in India

Physical Performance of Economic Assistance to SHGs

The physical performance of economic assistance to SHGs under SGSY in India is given in Table 4.8 and Fig. 4.8.

The number of SHGs Swarozgaris assisted was 26,14,714 in 2004-2005 and it was only 3,47,912 at the inception of SGSY in India. Similarly, the economic assistance to individual swarozgaries was 5,85,956 in the year 1999-2000 and it was 29,47,339 as on March 2005. The total Swarozgaris assisted during the past six year period was 65,62,053 in India. The percentage of SHGs Swarozgaries assisted was only 47.34 per cent during the six year period.

Economic Assistance for Swarozgaries in India

The physical performance of economic assistance for swarozgaries in India is analysed in Table 4.9 and Fig. 4.9.

It is clear that 2439776 SC/ST Swarozgaries were assisted under the SGSY scheme in India during the study period. Of the total SC/ST beneficiaries, 16,32,660 (66.92%) Swarozgaries belonged to the Scheduled Caste and 8,07,116 (33.08%) Swarozgaries belonged to the Scheduled Tribes in India.

The percentage of SC/ST assisted to the total economic assistance beneficiaries was 43.97. The total women Swarozgaries assisted under SGSY during the same period was 2538903. The growth performance shows that the number of women Swarozgaries was 416690 in the year 1999-2000 and it increased to 25,38,903 in the year 2004-2005. The percentage of women assisted was 45.77. The number of disabled Swarozgaries assisted under SGSY increased from 8529 in the year 1999-2000 to 7111 Swarozgaries in the year 2004-2005. The percentage of disabled assistance under the scheme was 7.24 during the six year period.

Table 4.8. Performance of Economic Assistance to SHGs Under SGSY in India

(In Nos.)

Sl. No.	Items	1999-2000	2000-2001	2001-2002	2002-2003	2003-2004	2004-2005	Total / Average
1.	SHGs Swarozgaris Assisted	347912	318803	364676	414419	572092	596812	2614714
2.	Individual Swaroggaris Assisted	585956	687349	572792	411848	303598	385796	2947339
3.	Total Swarozgaris Assisted	933868	1006152	937468	826267	875690	1982608	6562053
	Percentage of SHGs Swarozgaris Assisted	37.25	31.69	38.9	50.16	65.33	60.74	47.34

Source: Ministry of Rural Development, New Delhi, 2006.

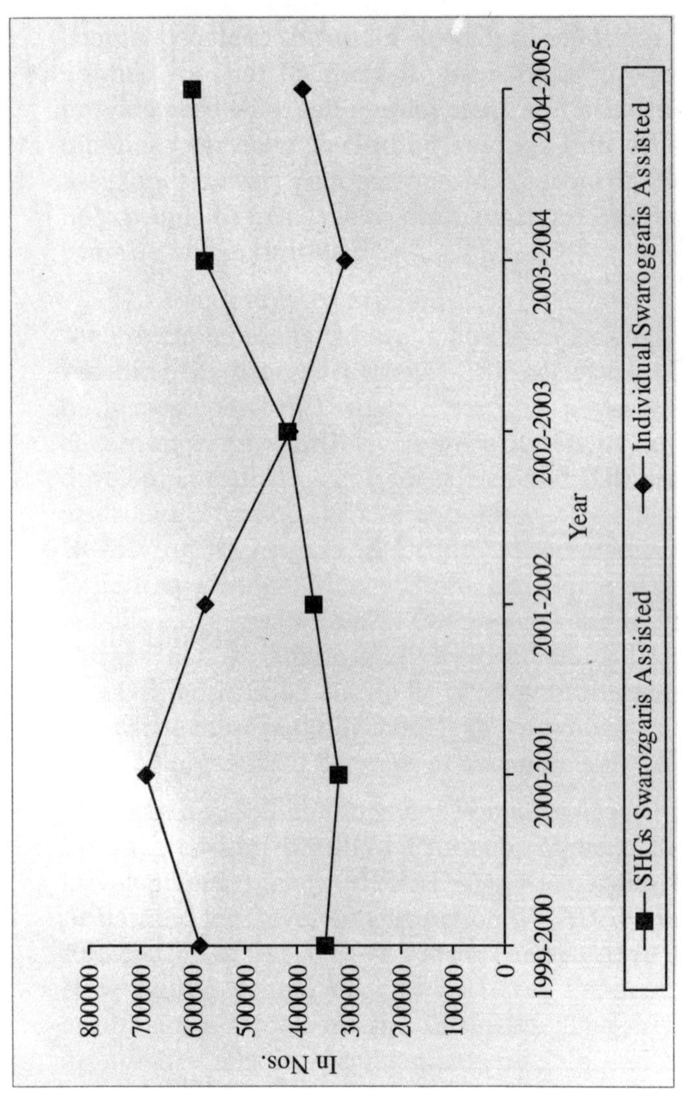

Fig. 4.8. Performance of Economic Assistance to SHGs Under SGSY in India

Table 4.9. Economic Assistance for Swarozgaries in India

(In Nos.)

Sl. No.	Items	1999-2000	2000-2001	2001-2002	2002-2003	2003-2004	2004-2005	Total / Average
1.	SC Swarozgaries Assisted	278938	310886	284040	249556	265959	243281	1632660
2.	ST Swarozgaries Assisted	134944	137850	143619	130260	135183	125260	807116
3.	Total SC/ST Swarozgaries Assisted	413882	448736	427659	379816	401142	368541	2439776
4.	Women Swarozgaries Assisted	416690	409842	385891	382613	462230	481637	2538903
5.	Disabled Swarozgaries Assisted	8529	6737	6059	6118	8316	7111	42870
6.	Percentage of SC/STs Assisted	44.32	44.6	45.62	45.97	45.81	37.51	43.97
7.	Percentage of Women Assisted	44.62	40.73	41.16	46.31	52.78	49.02	45.77
8.	Percentage of Disabled Assisted	0.91	0.67	0.65	0.74	0.95	7.24	1.86

Source: Ministry of Rural Development, New Delhi, 2006.

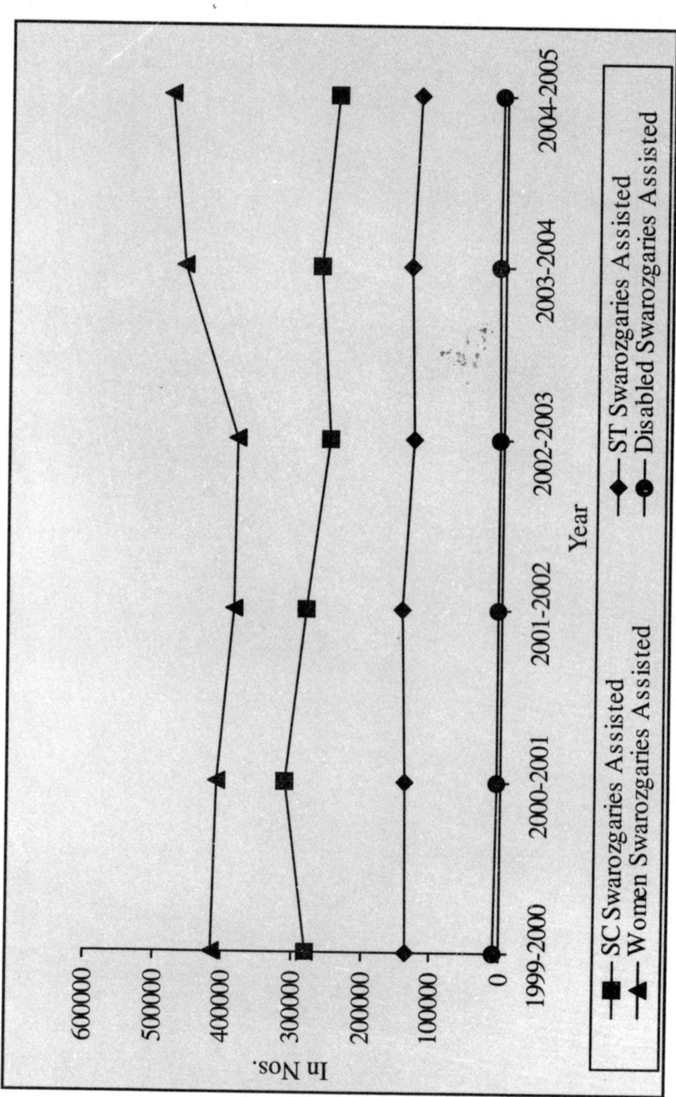

Fig. 4.9. Economic Assistance for Swarozgaries in India

LINKAGES OF SHGS AND MICRO-FINANCE INSTITUTIONS

Emergence of Micro-Credit

Rural credit was recognised as early as 1793 in India when regulation for taccavi loans to farmers and subordinate tenants for various purposes were issued, primarily aimed at regulating money-lending activities to reduce the indebtedness of the rural poor and provide solutions for it.[1] Literature suggests that by the 1850s it was found in Europe (Aghion-Murdoch, 2005). With regard to the current scenario, I quote Vijay Mahajan, who says:

> "There are 110 million agricultural holdings in India. A vast majority are small farms. About 80 per cent are below 5 acres. There are 35 million non-farm enterprises comprising household industries like weaving and service enterprises like cycle repair shops etc. So that makes 145 million productive enterprises. If each of them needs, let's suppose, only Rs.10,000 as working capital then you come to a number close to Rs.145,000 crore. That's the level of credit required. Some of this is already going to large farmers. For example, total credit from all the banks last year to rural India was around Rs.70,000 crore, including credit from cooperative banks."

The problem is that over half of this amount goes to large farmers and the access by small farmers is not adequate. To compare the Rs.70,000 crore supply with the working capital demand of Rs.145,000 crore itself shows that the system is already starved even for working capital. In addition, most of these farms and enterprises are under-capitalized in terms of lack of adequate irrigation or power or equipment. These enterprises need more support to grow. Therefore, actual financial requirement per holding comes to approximately Rs.50,000. The annual average credit usage per household from all sources worked out to Rs.14,549. Of this, 65 per cent was for productive purposes.

Long-term productive purpose, viz., purchase of livestock, farm machinery etc., accounted for 16 per cent of the total usage while the remaining 49 per cent was for short-term purposes like agriculture crop loan. Of the total usage, 35 per cent was for consumption purposes – 15 per cent being on account of long term purposes like house building, marriage, etc., and 20 per cent was for short-term purposes like house building, marriage, etc., and 20 per cent was for short-term purposes like household expenses, clothes, consumer durables and so on. According to the Reserve Bank of India (RBI) mid-term credit policy review, the linking of Self-help Groups (SHGs) with the banking system continues to be the major micro-finance programme in the country and is being implemented by commercial banks, RRBs and co-operative banks.

By end July 2005, as many as 16,53,047 SHGs were linked to banks and the total flow of credit to SHGs was Rs.7,063 crore. According to the World Bank estimate for 1998, almost 1,198 million people, world wide, are living in poverty. Of this, 522 million live in South Asia alone. It is estimated that women account for approximately half the world's population and over two-thirds of the world's poorest people. Poverty, in both developed and developing countries, has a predominantly female face.

India is currently facing a critical position-enjoying on the one hand, a remarkable period of economic growth in many sectors, yet at the same time trying to cope with more than 300 million people living below the poverty line, the highest concentration of poverty in any country in the world. Today, there still exists a massive gap between the demand for credit by poor households and the supply of credit by formal financial and social institutions. The dependence of rural poor on informal and non-institutional sources of credit still remains very high. Poverty continues to be a major concern despite reduction in the poverty ratio in the country from 55 per cent in 1973-74 to 36 per cent in 1993-94, viewed in the backdrop of the burgeoning population.

Group Approach

The main advantage of the group approach, according to Varena, accrues from economies of scale. Providing development services to individual small-scale farmers is too expensive for most governments. Small SHGs overcome this problem because they represent may farmers, not just one. When they deal with a group, development services are more efficient and have greater impact. For example: an extension agent can train many farmers at a single meeting: (*a*) Banks can provide one big loan for the season instead of many small ones; the group can take over responsibility for distributing fertilizers and seeds; (*b*) More production and income. Given better access to credit, inputs and information, the poor can achieve higher levels of production and income. Increased income creates savings, which can then be used to expand production even further and to meet other needs; (*c*) Acquisition of new skills. In a small group, the poor learn very quickly how to work together, analyse problems together and plan together. These are important skills that can be used in the development, at a later time, of inter-group federations and national-level organizations; and d) Sustainability. Small groups help the poor become more self-reliant and can be linked to a network of self-sustaining rural organizations. This carries important benefits – the increased efficiency of development services stimulates economic growth in rural areas and overall national development; politically, participation allows the poor to contribute constructively to development.

Self-help Groups (SHGs) have been defined differently by different organizations, researchers and practioners based on the required development activities. For example, Malcolm Harper (2002), Dhan Foundations (1998), NABARD (1997), Langsun T. Mate, D. Rai and Durga mangar (2002) have defined the concept differently. The SHGs are formed for watershed management, natural management, promotion of adult literacy or purely for the purpose of micro-financing. However, when we talk of the sustainability of micro-finance services, sustainable livelihood promotion, creating and building of people's institutions or MFIs, the definitions used somehow lack the feature of sustainability, empowerment and poverty alleviation. Therefore, there is a need to take a fresh look at the concept for sustainable micro-finance and enterprises.

Based on the literature available, the concept of the modern SHGs in India emerged from the work of organizations such as SEWA Bank, PRADAN and MYRADA. The experiences of these organizations and that of others, gleaned from various articles and books, have been reviewed in the process of developing this document.

According to MYRADA, SHGs came into existence way back in the Eighties. Fernandez wrote, "The first path began in 1984 when the first set of self-help affinity groups emerged spontaneously when the larger cooperatives organized by Myrada broke down due to conflict. By 1986 MYRADA had formed about 300 groups and approached NABARD for an R&D grant to start the pilot experiment to assess whether the groups could function as genuine institutions with functions that went beyond savings and credit. It was initially called the "Credit Management Group" approach by MYRADA since the focus was on 'Management' as an empowering tool. When NABARD started supporting this initiative in 1987, the name of the model changed to 'Self-help Groups'. When the Government of India decided to officially accept this model in 1998-1999, MYRADA decided to change the name to Self-help Affinity Groups to highlight the critical importance of 'affinity' as a binding force.

It was in 1999 that the Government of India officially recognized SHGs based on the NABARD-MYRADA experiment. Nevertheless, the first form of professionally managed micro-finance services emerged with Vijay Mahajan (PRADAN and now BASIX) in the late eighties. Basics initiated the concepts of Joint Liability Groups, Customer Service agents and micro-finance agents through which it provided loans to the poor and entrepreneurs as early as 1992.

Linkages

The NABARD, in partnership with various stakeholders, is facilitation SHG-Bank linkage Programme to enable the banking system to transcend the confines of supply driven savings and credit delivery mechanisms, which was neither cost effective for the banks, nor user-friendly for the poor. The programme provides a 'savings and credit history' for the poor. The programme provides a 'savings and credit history' for the members of the SHG, auguring well at the time of taking loans from the banks. Simultaneously, it helped the banks in reducing their transaction as well as risk cost in delivering small loans. On account of these positive features, the SHG-Bank linkage programme caught the imagination of not only the financial institutions, but governmental and non-governmental agencies also joined hands with NABARD in its efforts. Today, this unique initiative in India of more than 3,024 partners has blossomed into the fastest growing and the most cost effective micro-finance initiative in the world, enabling 16.7 million poor families to access sustainable financial services from the banking system, through a network of over one million SHGs.

A significant development, which has far-reaching positive impact on the SHG-Bank linkage, is the growing involvement of local and state governments and the branches of banks, especially RRBs and DCCBs, in promotion of SHGs. With the help of their large presence at the field level, they assisted in formation and nurturing of 959,815 SHGs as on March 2004. Some State Governments also took steps to accept SHG-Bank linkage norms or benchmarking quality thresholds for similar programmes led by them, thereby adding value to their poverty alleviation initiatives. The informal sector comprising the NGOs and other local agencies of varying sizes and outreach capabilities also significantly contributed to these efforts, by forming and nurturing 557,745 SHGs as on March 2004.

The value addition to SHG-Bank linkage programme from NABARD continued to be significant during the year, in the form of initiatives in developing and sharing different levels of conceptual and capacity building inputs with the stakeholders. These efforts were supplemented by the financial support to its partners from NABARD. As a part of its training strategy, NABARD organized and funded national and international exposure visits for officials from partner agencies. The intellectual inputs for training of bankers, government officials and NGOs in formation and credit linking SHGs were developed in consultation with banks and NGOs in formation and credit linking SHGs were developed in consultation with banks and NGOs, and were widely circulated in print form to all partners. In addition, the audio-visual training supplement in multimedia format developed last year (2002-03) has been dubbed into some local languages for wider use by the capacity building units of the partner agencies.

The circulation of micro-finance newsletters *'Saving Grace'* and *'Akshay Patra'* have been stepped up from 10,000 to 40,000 copies each by NABARD to cover a larger segment of partners for experience sharing and for spreading of best practices among the practitioners of micro-finance. These measures, funded from the Micro-finance Development Fund (MFDF) held by NABARD, were found useful in enhancing the effectiveness of the staff of banks, NGOs and government agencies at the grassroot level. The Government of India (GOI) and the Reserve Bank of India (RBI) espoused these initiatives with appropriate and conductive policy support, leading to the rapid progress in the micro-finance initiatives of the agencies involved in it. External support for value addition to NABARD's initiatives came from the Swiss Agency for Development Cooperation (SDC) and the German Agency for Technical Collaboration (GTC).

The formal financial sector comprising commercial banks (CBs), regional rural banks (RRBs) and the cooperative banks (COOPs) carved out a niche for themselves in micro-finance, by scaling up the credit flow to SHGs during 2003-04 to Rs.18,555 million (US$ 412 million), which nearly equalled the cumulative bank loans given to SHGs from 1992 up to March 2003 (Rs.20,487 million or US$ 455 million). These were small loans without any collateral security, with an average size of Rs.2,412 per family, made available to 16.7 million families who did not get a sustained service from the banking system earlier. The banks are free to decide on their lending rates to SHGs. At present, the interest rates charged by banks to SHGs generally range from 8 per cent to 12 per cent per annum.

The grant support from NABARD to all partner agencies during 2003-04 for promoting and nurturing SHGs and for capacity building at different levels of partner agencies aggregated to Rs.82.77 million (US $ 1.84 million). Apart from this, the refinance support extended by NABARD to the financing banks was in the order of Rs.7,054 million (US $ 157 million).

The performance of banks in linking SHGs to the banking system scaled enviable heights during the year. The banks financed 361,731 new SHGs during 2003-04 (2,55,882 SHGs during 2002-03). The cumulative number of SHGs credit linked with banks increased to 1,079,091 as on 31 March 2004 covering more than 16.7 million poor households as against 7,17,360 SHGs covering 11.6 million poor households as on 31 March 2003. NABARD had set a mission of credit linking one million SHGs by 2007 and the mission was achieved 3 years ahead of the schedule.

Total bank loans disbursed to SHGs during the year aggregated to Rs.18,555 million (including repeat loans of Rs.6,978 million provided to 1,71,669 existing SHGs already financed in earlier years) as compared to Rs.10,224 million disbursed during the previous year, registering a growth of

82 per cent over the previous year. Though cent percent refinance from NABARD was available at all banks for SHG lending, some banks did not utilize the facility to the full extent.

SHG-Bank Linkage-Cumulative Progress (1992-2004)

Table 4.10 and Fig. 4.10 shows the SHG-Bank Linkage-Cumulative Progress.

Table 4.10. SHG-Bank Linkage-Cumulative Progress (1992-2004)

Up to End March	SHGs Financed	Bank Loan (Rs. in Million)
1992-1999	32,995	571
1999-2000	114,775	1,930
2000-2001	263,825	4,809
2001-2002	461,478	10,263
2002-2003	717,360	20,487
2003-2004	1,079,091	39,042

Source: NABARD, Mumbai, 2006.

It is clear from the Table 4.10 the bank loans aggregating Rs.39042 million were disbursed to 1,079,091 SHGs with refinance support of Rs.21242 million from NABARD up to 31st March 2004. Around 90 per cent of the SHGs linked were exclusive women SHGs.

Positive Trends in Cumulative Growth in SHGs-Linked to Banks

The positive growth of SHG-Bank linkage in some of the regions and States indicated in Table 4.11 was facilitated by the state and region-specific strategies developed by NABARD in consultation with its Regional Offices at the State level, banks, NGOs and the State Governments.

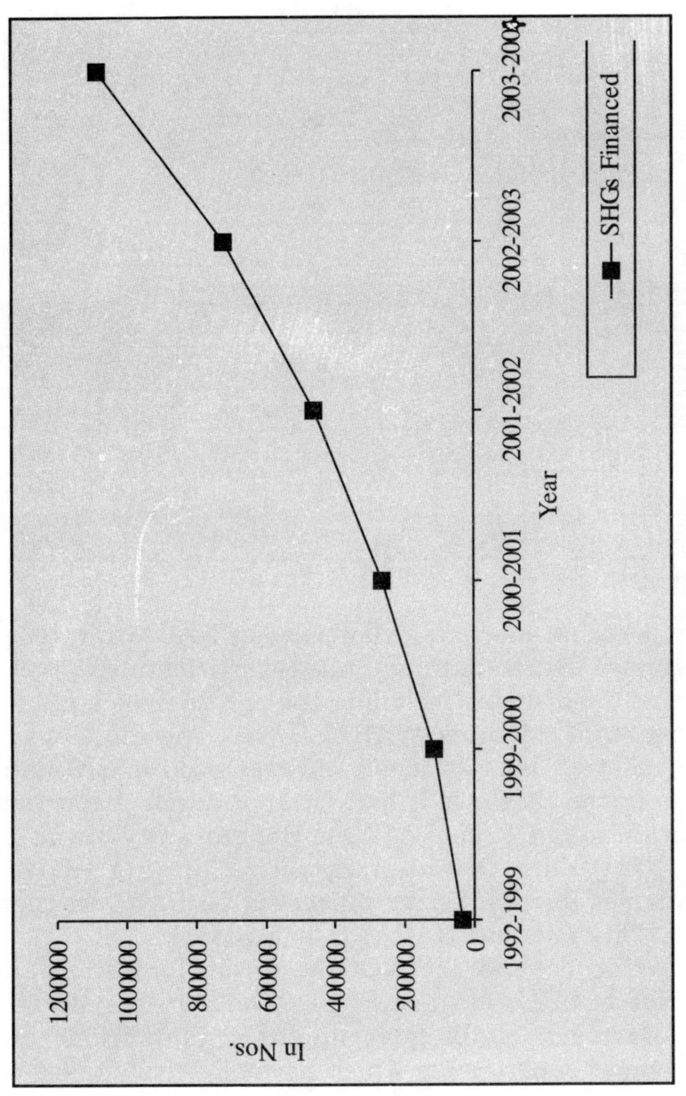

Fig. 4.10. SHG-Bank Linkage-Cumulative Progress (1992-2004)

Table 4.11 shows the Positive Trends in Cumulative Growth in SHGs-Linked to Banks.

Table 4.11. Positive Trends in Cumulative Growth in SHGs Linked to Banks

Region/State	March 1999	March 2000	March 2001	March 2002	March 2003	March 2004
NE Region	93	196	477	1,490	4,069	12,278
KBK Region	526	1,425	4,192	9,869	18,934	31,732
Orissa	2,018	4,068	8,888	20,553	42,272	77,588
Bihar	496	1,910	4,592	3,957	8,161	16,246
Jharkhand	—	—	—	4,198	7,765	12,647
Uttar Pradesh	2,812	12,953	23,152	33,114	53,696	79,210
Uttrakhand	—	—	—	3,323	5,853	10,908
Rajasthan	710	1,941	5,616	12,564	22,742	33,846
Madhya Pradesh	733	2,303	5,699	7,981	15,271	27,095
Chhattisgarh	—	—	—	-3,763	-6,763	-9,796
All India	**32,995**	**114,775**	**263,825**	**461,478**	**717,360**	**1,079.091**

Source: NABARD, 2006.

Promotional efforts were launched by NABARD through its Regional Offices in these States, participating agencies and other institutions including the government and non-governmental agencies. NABARD took specific steps to identify district level bottlenecks in expansion of SHG-Bank linkage in the States of Bihar, Uttar Pradesh, Rajasthan, Assam, Madhya Pradesh, West Bengal and Orissa, by conducting Goal Oriented Project Planning (GOPP) programmes for the district officers of NABARD in these states. This enabled NABARD to widen its network of partnership beyond the NGO sector in formation and nurturing of SHGs in these States. The partners included RRBs, farmers' clubs, government organizations and development departments which have effectively taken up the role of promoting and nurturing SHGs. Almost all commercial (48), RRBs (196) and co-operatives (316) participated in SHG-Bank linkage.

SHG-Bank Linkage Programme – Highlights

The study shows that there is eight times growth in the case of SHGs provided with bank loan during the five years period. The percentage of women groups participation also increased from 85 to 90 per cent.

Table 4.12 shows the SHG-Bank Linkage Programme – Highlights.

Table 4.12. SHG-Bank Linkage Programme – Highlights March 2001 to March 2004

(Rs. in Million)

Sl. No.	Items	March 2000	March 2001	March 2002	March 2003	March 2004
1.	No. of new SHGs provided with bank loan	81780	149050	197653	255882	361731
2.	No. of SHGs provided with bank loan	114775	263825	461478	717360	1079091
3.	Percentage of Women groups	85	90	90	90	90
4.	No. of participating banks	266	314	444	505	560
	Commercial Banks	40	43	44	48	48
	Regional Rural Banks	165	177	191	192	196
	Co-operative banks	61	94	209	265	316
5.	No. of States/Uts	24	27	30	30	31
6.	No. of districts covered	362	412	488	502	563
7.	No. of NGOs	718	1030	2155	2800	3024
8.	Bank Loan (cumulative)	1930	4809	10263	20487	39042
9.	Refinance (cumulative)	1501	4007	7965	14188	21247
10.	No. of families assisted (in million)	1.9	4.5	7.8	11.6	16.7
11.	Average Loan / SHG (Rs)	16814	18227	22240	28559	36179
12.	Average Loan / Family (Rs.)	1016	1072	1316	1766	2412
13.	Model-wise linkage (cumulative)					
	SHGs formed and financed by banks	14%	13%	16%	20%	20%
	SHGs formed by formal agencies and NGOs	70%	76%	75%	72%	72%
	SHGs financed by banks through NGOs	16%	11%	9%	8%	8%

Source: NABARD, 2006.

Table 4.12 shows that there is positive growth in the SHGs-Bank linkage programmes in India during the study period. The number of new SHGs provided with bank increased from 81,780 in 1999-2000 to 3,61,731 in 2003-2004. Similarly, the number of SHGs provided with bank loan also increased from 1,14,775 in 1999-2000 to 10,79,091 in 2003-2004. In 1999-2000, only 266 banks participated in the linkage of SHGs and it had doubled (560) in the year 2003-2004.

SHG-Bank Linkage Programme – Southern Regional Spread of Physical and Financial Progress as on 31 March 2004

It is clear that the cumulative Bank loan to the SHGs up to 31 March 2004, was Rs. 39,042.08 million in India. In Tamil Nadu State, the cumulative Bank loan to the SHGs up to 31st March 2004 was Rs. 9,314.25 (23.86%).

Table 4.13 shows the SHG-Bank Linkage Programme – southern regional spread of physical and financial progress.

Table 4.13. SHG-Bank Linkage Programme – Southern Regional Spread of Physical and Financial Progress as on 31 March 2004

(Rs. in Million)

Sl. No.	Region/ State	Cumulative Number of SHGs provided with bank loan upto 31 March 2003	No. of SHGs provided with bank loan during 2003-04	Up to 31 March 2004	Provided with bank loan during 2003-2004	Bank loan 2003-2004	Cumulative bank loan upto 31 March 2004
1.	Andhra Pradesh	281338	104238	385576	9753.87	7529.92	17283.79
2.	Karnataka	62178	41688	103866	1440.14	1396.04	2836.18
3.	Kerala	21012	12716	33728	644.87	584.19	1229.06
4.	Tamil Nadu	98410 (13.72)	51851 (14.33)	150261 (13.92)	4255.16 (20.77)	5059.09 (27.26)	9314.25 (23.86)
5.	UT of Pondicherry	774	151	925	40.2	35.73	75.93
	Total Southern Region	463712	210644	674356	16134.24	14604.97	30739.21
6.	India	717360	361731	1079091	20486.77	18555.31	39042.08

Source: NABARD, 2006.

Table 4.13 reveals the SHG-Bank linkage programme – Regional spread of physical and financial progress as on 31 March 2004. It shows that there is a greater participation of the SHGs and the banks in lending loans. Similarly, the cumulative number of SHGs provided with bank loan up to 31st March 2004 was 10,79,091 in India and in Tamil Nadu alone, 1,50,261 (13.92%) SHGs were provided with bank loan up to 31st March 2004.

SHG-Bank Linkage Agency-wise Cumulative Participation

The NABARD has been instrumental in the formation and nurturing of quality SHGs by means of promotional grant support to NGOs, RRBs, DCCBs, Farmers Club of individual volunteers and in developing capacity building of various partners, which have brought about excellent results in the promotion of SHGs. Further, increasing number of partner institutions functioning as Self-Help promoting Institution (SHPI) resulted in the expansion of the programme throughout the country. The financial support provided by NABARD to its partner institutions and their progress in SHGs promotion linkage is given in Table 4.14.

The local character and regional spread of RRBs give them an advantage in providing promotional and nurturing support to SHGs. Therefore, NABARD has been encouraging RRBs for this purpose from 1999 onwards up to 31 March 2004. In India, 4,05,998 SHGs got loan assistance of Rs.12,782.58 million from the Regional Rural Banks. In Tamil Nadu, during the same period, 39,894 (9.83 percent) SHGs got loan assistance of Rs.2,256.98 million (17.66%).

The NABARD has been supporting capacity building, exposure and awareness creation institutions of the cooperatives to mainstream SHGs-Bank linkage in the cooperative banking sector. During the same period, the Tamil Nadu State SHGs got the loan assistance of Rs.5,892.3 million (26.13%).

Table 4.14. SHG-Bank Linkage Agency-wise Cumulative Participation up to 31st March 2004

(Rs. in Million)

Sl. No.	Region/State	Commercial Banks		Regional Banks		Cooperative Banks		Total	
		No. of SHGs (Rs.)	Bank Loan (Rs.)	No. of SHGs (Rs.)	Bank Loan (Rs.)	No. of SHGs (Rs.)	Bank Loan (Rs.)	No. of SHGs (Rs.)	Bank Loan (Rs.)
1.	Andhra Pradesh	246123	11426	130470	5546.91	8983	310.84	385576	17283.8
2.	Karnataka	38605	1006.79	37087	1094.73	28174	734.66	103866	2836.18
3.	Kerala	21378	785.91	5365	135.72	6985	307.43	33728	1229.06
4.	Tamil Nadu & Puducheery UT	(16.06) 6463	(26.13) 5892.3	(9.83) 39894	(17.66) 2256.98	(18.44) 24829	(33.44) 1240.9	(14.01) 151186	(24.05) 9390.19
5.	India	538,422	22548.29	405,998	12782.58	134,671	3,711.21	1,079,091	39,042.08
	Total	392569	19111	212816	9034.34	68971	2593.8	674356	30739.2

Source: NABARD, 2006.

The contribution of commercial banks up to 31st march 2004 in providing loan assistance was Rs. 22,548.29 million to the 5,38,422 SHGs in India. At the national level, the cooperative banks provided loan assistance to 134.671 SHGs to the extent of Rs.3711.21 million upto 31st March 2004. In Tamil Nadu, the 24,829 SHGs got loan assistance of Rs.1240.90 million from the cooperative banks.

The SHG-Bank Linkage – Physical and Financial Progress of Commercial Banks

The SHG-Bank Linkage-physical and financial progress of Commercial Banks (Public Sector Banks) upto 31st March is explained in Table 4.15.

Table 4.15. SHG-Bank Linkage – Physical and Financial Progress of Commercial Banks up to 31 March 2004 (Public Sector Banks)

(Rs. in Million)

Sl. No.	Commercial Banks	Cumulative No. of SHGs provided with Bank Loan upto 31 March 204	Cumulative Bank Loan disbursed upto 31 March 2004 (Rs.)
1.	Allahabad Bank	6523	140.65
2.	Andhra Bank	81581	3641.8
3.	Bank of Baroda	19219	543.65
4.	Bank of India	20398	610.78
5.	Bank of Maharashtra	6243	183.56
6.	Canara Bank	25715	928.04
7.	Corporation Bank	7635	229.26
8.	Central Bank of India	12244	490.24
9.	Dena Bank	2690	40.33
10.	Indian Bank	47212	2446.99

...(Contd.)

11.	Indian Overseas Bank	31478	1115.29
12.	Oriental Bank of Commerce	6219	182.67
13.	Punjab & Sind Bank	389	17.18
14.	Punjab National Bank	11427	410.43
15.	State Bank of India	131738	5487.01
16.	State Bank of Bikaner & Jaipur	1760	41.73
17.	State Bank of Hyderabad	35591	1327.32
18.	State Bank of Indore	2480	77.52
19.	State Bank of Mysore	2495	87.98
20.	State Bank of Patiala	541	28.59
21.	State Bank of Saurashtra	1313	14.56
22.	State Bank of Travancore	3682	134.57
23.	Syndicate Bank	19236	899.46
24.	Union Bank of India	15383	604.2
25.	United Bank of India	7543	75.07
26.	UCO Bank	7015	162.55
27.	Vijaya Bank	8947	274.02
	Total	516697	20195.45

Source: NABARD, 2006.

Regarding the total loan assistance, the public sector banks play a better role than the private sector banks. Of the loan assistance, public sector banks had disbursed Rs. 20,195.45 million (89.57%) to the 516,697 SHGs (95.97%) up to March 2004.

SHG-Bank Linkage – Physical and Financial Progress of Commercial Banks upto 31 March 2004 (Private Sector Banks)

Table 4.16 shows the physical and financial progress of private sector banks up to 31st March 2004.

Table 4.16. SHG-Bank Linkage – Physical and Financial Progress of Commercial Banks upto 31 March 2004 (Private Sector Banks)

(Rs. in Million)

Sl. No.	Commercial Banks	Cumulative No. of SHGs provided with Bank Loan up to 31 March 2004	Cumulative Bank Loan disbursed up to 31 March 2004 (Rs.)
1.	Sangi Bank Limited	137	2.79
2.	Bank Rajasthan Limited	992	12.06
3.	Dhanalaxmi Bank Limited	888	25.18
4.	Global Trust Bank Limited	867	16.20
5.	Jammu & Kashmir Bank Ltd.	153	2.98
6.	Karnataka Bank Ltd.	975	28.85
7.	South Indian Bank Ltd.	901	36.50
8.	Tamilnadu Mercantile Bank Ltd.	280	4.65
9.	Vysya Bank Ltd.	5091	177.96
10.	Catholic Syrian Bank Ltd.	315	4.59
11.	Federal Bank Ltd.	854	29.68
12.	Lord Krishna Bank Ltd.	42	2.43
13.	City Union Bank Ltd.	479	9.70
14.	Laxmi Vilas Bank Ltd.	450	10.36
15.	Karur Vysya Bank Ltd.	241	6.19
16.	ICICI Bank Ltd.	8021	1933.75
17.	National Bank Ltd.	99	5.87
18.	The United Western Bank Ltd.	64	1.79
19.	Ratnakar Bank Ltd.	13	0.07
20.	UTI Bank Ltd.	328	20.00
21.	K.B.S. Local Area Bank	535	21.24
	Total	21725	2352.84

Source: NABARD, 2006.

From Table 4.16 it is clear that the private sector banks provided loan assistance to 21,725 SHGs and disbursed bank loan Rs. 2352.84 million up to 31st March 2004.

SHG-Bank Linkage by Commercial Banks in India up to 31st March 2004

Table 4.17 shows SHG-Banks Linkage-physical and financial progress of commercial banks in India upto 31st March 2004.

Table 4.17. SHG-Bank Linkage by Commercial Banks in India upto 31 March 2004

(Rs. in Million)

Sl. No.	Details up to 31st March, 2004	Private Sector Banks	Public Sector Banks	Total
1.	Cumulative Number of SHGs provided with Bank Loan	21725 (4.03)	516,697 (95.97)	538,422 (100)
2.	Cumulative Bank Loan disbursed (Rs.)	2352.84 (10.43)	20,195.45 (89.57)	22548.29 (100)

Source: NABARD, 2006.
Note: Figures within parentheses denotes percentages.

Commercial banks in India provided cumulative loan assistance of Rs.538,422 million and disbursed Rs. 22,548.29 million.

SHG-Bank Linkage-Physical and Financial Progress of Participating Regional Rural Banks

Table 4.18 shows the SHG-Bank Linkage-Physical and Financial Progress of Participating Regional Rural Banks.

Southern Region of NABARD includes the states of Andhra Pradesh, Karnataka, Tamil Nadu and Pondicherry Union Territory. The SHG-Bank Linkage-physical and financial progress of participating Regional Rural Banks up to 31st March 2004 in Tamil Nadu State and union territory of Puducherry is analysed in Table 4.18. The Regional Rural

Banks in the southern region includes the Adhiyaman Grama Bank, Pandiyan Grama Bank and the Vallalar Grama Bank. It is clear that the Regional Rural Banks had provided the loan assistance of Rs.2256.98 million to the total of 39894 SHGs in Tamil Nadu and Puducherry.

Table 4.18. SHG-Bank Linkage – Physical and Financial Progress of Participating Regional Rural Banks upto 31 March 2004 (Tamil Nadu and Union Territory of Puducherry)

(Rs. in million)

Sl. No.	Name of the RRB	Cumulative No. of SHGs provided with Bank Loan upto 31 March 2004	Cumulative Bank Loan disbursed upto 31 March 2004 (Rs.)
1.	Adhiyaman Grama Bank	3532	395.49
2.	Pandiyan Grama Bank	33169	1758.47
3.	Vallalar Grama Bank	3193	103.02
4.	Total 1 + 2 + 3	39894	2256.98
5.	India	405998	12782.58
6.	Total (4 + 5)	445892	15029.56

Source: NABARD, 2006.

SHG-Bank Linkage by Co-operative Banks

Table 4.19 shows the SHG-Bank Linkage – physical and financial progress of participating Co-operative Banks.

Table 4.19 reveals the SHG-Bank Linkage – physical and financial progress of participating Co-operative Banks up to 31st March 2004.

It is clear from Table 4.19 that the SHG-Bank Linkage performance was very well in the Tiruchirappalli district of Tamil Nadu state followed by the Kumbakonam district (2nd Bank). The poor performance districts are Sivagangai,

Vellore and Tirunelveli. The Kanyakumari district secured the 15th rank in the financial performance upto 31st March 2004.

Table 4.19. SHG-Bank Linkage – Physical and Financial Progress of Participating Co-operative Banks upto 31 March 2004

(Rs. in Million)

Sl. No.	Commercial Banks	Cumulative No. of SHGs provided with Bank Loan upto 31 March 2004	Cumulative Bank Loan disbursed upto 31 March 2004 (Rs.)
1	2	3	4
1.	Coimbatore DCCB	510	1181 (0.95)
2.	Cuddalore DCCB	1488	57.33 (4.62)
3.	Dharmapuri DCCB	1191	124.5 (10.03)
4.	Dindigul DCCB	905	26.36 (2.12)
5.	Erode DCCB	886	50.65 (4.08)
6.	Kancheepuram DCCB	675	21.24 (1.71)
7.	Kanyakumari DCCB	815	74.31 (5.99)
8.	Kumbakonam DCCB	2576	57.37 (4.62)
9.	Madurai DCCB	519	43.09 (3.47)
10.	Nilgiris DCCB	1059	23.34 (1.88)
11.	Pudukottai DCCB	1040	68.48 (5.52)

...(Contd.)

1	2	3	4
12.	Ramnad DCCB	897	93.61 (7.54)
13.	Salem DCCB	1153	85.15 (6.86)
14.	Sivagangai DCCB	240	16.15 (1.30)
15.	Thanjavur DCCB	2324	65.07 (5.24)
16.	Tiruchirappalli DCCB	3777	123.18 (9.93)
17.	Tirunelveli DCCB	399	32.29 (2.60)
18.	Tiruvannamalai DCCB	949	68.16 (5.49)
19.	Tuticorin DCCB	724	27.22 (2.19)
20.	Vellore DCCB	341	14.51 (1.17)
21.	Villupuram DCCB	1193	69.87 (5.63)
22.	Virudunagar DCCB	1168	87.21 (7.03)
	Total	24829	1240.90 (100)

Source: NABARD, 2006.
Note: Figures within parentheses denote percentages.

SHG-Bank Linkage – District-wise Cumulative and Financial Progress

Table 4.20 shows the district-wise cumulative and financial progress upto 31st March 2004.

Table 4.20 reveals the SHG-Bank Linkage – District-wise cumulative physical and financial progress up to 31st March 2004. It is clear from the Table that the SHG-Bank linkage performance was very well in the Dharmapuri District of Tamil Nadu State, followed by the Tirunelveli District (2nd Bank). The performance was poor in Theni, Tiruvellore, Perambalore, Karur, Erode and Coimbatore Districts. The Kanyakumari District secured the 21st rank in the financial performance up to 31st March 2004.

Table 4.20. SHG-Bank Linkage – District-wise Cumulative Physical and Financial Progress up to 31 March 2004

(Rs. in Million)

Sl. No.	Commercial Banks	Cumulative No. of SHGs provided with Bank Loan up to 31 March 2004	Cumulative Bank Loan disbursed up to 31 March 2004 (Rs.)	Bank
1	2	3	4	5
1.	Coimbatore	2106	123.43	22
2.	Cuddalore	4326	217.59	13
3.	Dharmapuri	14894	1552.81	1
4.	Dindigul	3620	173.78	19
5.	Erode	2574	153.67	23
6.	Kancheepuram	5878	188.52	18
7.	Kanyakumari	6526	168.14	21
8.	Karur	1302	44.04	27
9.	Madurai	7828	725.01	4
10.	Nagapattinam	4968	216.69	14
11.	Namakkal	3166	208.00	16
12.	Nilgiris	1999	61.83	26
13.	Perambalore	744	42.52	28
14.	Pudukottai	3699	441.47	7
15.	Ramanathapuram	7513	478.30	6

...(Contd.)

1	2	3	4	5
16.	Salem	5756	324.23	9
17.	Sivaganga	7921	773.04	3
18.	Thanjavur	4936	206.70	17
19.	Theni	661	65.78	25
20.	Thoothukudi	9111	505.70	5
21.	Tiruchirappalli	8672	277.44	11
22.	Tirunelveli	15952	1034.43	2
23.	Tiruvallore	1373	68.15	24
24.	Tiruvannamalai	3462	208.76	15
25.	Tiruvarur	3643	218.05	12
26.	Vellore	4408	169.30	20
27.	Villupuram	6417	301.86	10
28.	Virudhunagar	6806	365.00	8
	Total	150261	9314.25	

Source: NABARD, 2006.

SHG and Bank Linkages in India – 2004-05

Table 4.21 shows the SHG and Bank Linkage in India – 2004-05.

Table 4.21. SHG and Bank Linkages in India – 2004-05

Agency	During 2004-05			Cumulative as on 31.03.2005		
	Number	Amount (Rs. in Million)	For Promotion and Linkage of SHGs	Number	Amount (Rs. in Million)	For Promotion and Linkage of SHGs
NGOs	263	42.66	24234	1048	193.87	139513
RRBs	12	2.97	3890	93	30.55	38935
DCCBs	26	10.63	12560	55	23.03	28110

Note: RRB-Regional/Rural Bank; DCCB-District Central Cooperative Bank.

From Table 4.21 it is clear that 1048 NGOs provided loan assistance of Rs.193.87 million to 139513 SHGs, 93 RRBs provided loan assistance of Rs.30.55 million to 38935 SHGs and 55 DCCBs provided Rs.23.03 million to 28110 SHGs for the promotion and linkage activities.

SUMMARY

Micro-finance in 2004-05

The achievements of rural micro-finance during 2004-05 according to NABARD is given below:

Credit Operations

- Short-term credit limits sanctioned during 2004-05.
  - * For SCBs, RRBs - seasonal agricultural operations– Rs. 10185.06 crore
  - * For RRBs - other than seasonal agricultural operations – Rs. 216.83 crore
  - * For SCBs-financing Weavers' Cooperative Societies – Rs. 349.89 crore
- Long term loans sanctioned to seven state governments for contribution to the share capital of cooperative credit.
- Liquidity support to SCBs – 1914.24 crore.
- Liquidity support to RRBs – 158.78 crore.
- Investment Credit to CBs, SCARDBs, SCBs, RRBs and other eligible institutions – Rs.7605.29 crore.

Kisan Credit Card Scheme

- During the year (upto February 2005), 70.43 lakh cards were issued by cooperative banks, RRBs and commercial banks.
- Since inception in 1998-99, 4.84 crore cards were issued.

Rural Infrastructure Development Fund

- Goal announced Rs. 8000 crore for RIDF XI (2005-06)
- As at the end of March 2005, RIDF sanctions under all the branches of RIDF amounted to Rs. 42,948.51 crore against which the disbursements were Rs. 25384.02 crore.

SHG Bank Linkage Programme Highlights – 2004-05

- During the period April 2004 to March 2005 – 5,39,385 new SHGs were financed by banks to a tune of Rs.29.94 billion by way of loans.
- Cumulatively, banks have lent Rs.68.98 billion to 1,618,476 SHGs. 35,294 branches of 560 banks (Commercial Banks – 48; Regional Rural Banks – 196; and Cooperative Banks – 316) situated in 563 districts in the 30 States of the country are participating in the programme (Data-Provisional).
- About 24.25 million poor households have gained access to formal banking system through SHG-Bank linkage programme.
- Nearly 90 per cent of the groups are women-only groups.

Capacity Building Initiatives

Around 42,812 bank officials, 4246 NGO staff, 7063 government officials and 2,07,916 self-help group members trained with grant support from NABARD. In addition, about 161 faculty members of various banks were also trained cumulatively, 10,16,000 persons trained through various SHG related capacity-building programmes.

REFERENCE

1. Sinha, S.K., Rural Development through Bank Credit in India, Suneja Publishers, Delhi, 2000.

CHAPTER 5

Micro-Finance and Self-Help Group Members in Kanyakumari District

Introduction

The primary data were collected from 45 SHGs and the 225 individual beneficiaries of SGSY scheme in Kanyakumari (KK) district in the year 2005-2006. The collected data are presented in this chapter. The present chapter is divided into four sections. The first section reveals the profile of the sample respondents. The economic impact of micro-finance on the SHG members of SGSY scheme are analysed in the second section. The third section presents the data analysis with suitable statistical tools. The problems faced by the SGSY beneficiaries and the implementers are reviewed in the last section of the chapter.

PROFILE OF SAMPLE RESPONDENTS SELF-HELP GROUPS

The present study was conducted with the three types of SHGs in the study district. They are: (*i*) Direct Beneficiaries of SGSY, (*ii*) NGO facilitated groups and (*iii*) NGO served as intermediary groups. A sample of 15 SHGs in each category was selected for the study. The profile of the 45 sample SHGs are discussed in this part.

The average size of the group is 45. Small farmers constituted the major share of the number of members followed by agricultural labourers. It is clear that the farmers and agricultural labourers are effectively involved in SHG's formation due to the seasonal occupation in the agricultural sector and the problem of unemployment (Table 5.1).

Table 5.1. Average Size of the Group

Category	Models			Total
	Direct	NGO Facilitator	NGO Interme-diary	
Small farmers	6	7	6	19
Agricultural Labour	5	7	3	15
Petty trade	1	2	3	6
Non-farm activities	1	0	1	2
Artisans	1	0	2	3
Total	14	16	15	45

Source: Computed from Primary data.

Homogeneity of the Group

Homogeneity in terms of living together in the same village or having uniform standards of living and socio-economic conditions were the major factors influencing the cohesiveness of the groups. Table 5.2 shows the major criteria for group formation model.

Table 5.2. Major Criteria for Group Formation Model

Category	Models			Total
	Direct	NGO Facilitator	NGO Interme-diary	
Activity	10.4	6.6	16.3	11.10
Homogeneity in Standard of Living	58.2	67.1	48.8	58.03
Proximity of Residences	29.9	26.3	32.6	29.60
Miscellaneous	1.5	0.0	2.3	1.27
Total	100.0	100.0	100.0	100.00

Source: Computed from Primary data.

Homogeneity in the standard of living constituted the major factor (58.03%) followed by proximity of residences (29.60%). About 1.27 per cent of the groups were formed based on activities. Similar trend was observed among different models.

Conduct of Meetings

Regular meetings at fixed intervals in a common place is one of the core activities of the SHG during which they undertake financial transactions, both in terms of collection of savings and also disbursement of loans. In addition, this occasion is used to discuss their common problems and other issues that need to be sorted out through the intervention of the group or its members. Table 5.3 shows distribution of groups according to attendance.

Table 5.3. Distribution of Groups according to Attendance

Attendance (%)	No. of SHGs	Percentage of SHGs
30-49	2	4.44
50-69	3	6.67
70-89	12	26.67
90-99	14	31.11
100	14	31.11
Total	45	100.00

Source: Computed from Primary data.

The level of attendance and the frequency of the meetings may be judging the performance of the groups. About 62.22 per cent of the groups recorded more than 90 per cent attendance during the group meetings, which indicated the active involvement of the members.

Frequency of Meetings Organized by Groups Model

Table 5.4 shows the frequency of meetings organized by groups model.

Table 5.4. Frequency of Meetings Organized by Groups-Model

Category Model	Periodicity				Total
	Weekly	Fort-night	Monthly	Irregular	
Direct	25	16	57	2	100
NGO Facilitator	20	4	62	14	100
NGO Intermediary	26	33	36	5	100
Overall	23.67	17.67	51.67	7	100

Source: Computed from Primary data.

Arranging meeting on monthly basis was observed to be the common phenomena (51.67%) followed by weekly meetings (23.67%). Fortnightly meetings were organized by 17.67 per cent of the groups and in the case of about 7 per cent of the groups meetings were not regularly organized. Organizing monthly meeting was more frequent among model with NGOs as facilitator and the groups financed directly by the banks.

Savings

Savings formed one of the main products in the SHG-Bank linkage programme. The members contributed periodically, for instance, at weekly intervals, a pre-determined amount as savings. The amount of savings per member during a given period varied across the groups. Increase in this amount over time is often observed. Further, models with direct involvement of banks may have higher amount of periodical savings since banks normally show the tendency to build savings faster to form tangible collateral for their lending. Table 5.5 shows the source of funds of the SHGs.

The average savings per sample SHG during the year 2005-2006 worked out to Rs. 14461. The savings per group was relatively higher in SHGs formed directly by the banks (Rs. 22,381) when compared to the model with NGO as facilitator (Rs. 15,855) and Rs. 5,147 in model with NGO as intermediary. The trend in these averages would not change even if normalized with respect to the size of the groups across different categories as the size of groups was more or less the same.

Table 5.5. Source of Funds of the SHGs

Purpose	Models			Overall
	Direct	NGO Facilitator	NGO Interme-diary	
Savings	22381 (35.15)	15855 (37.34)	5147 (34.16)	14461 (35.95)
NGO Contributions	149 (0.24)	597 (1.40)	1202 (7.98)	576 (1.31)
Bank Loan	31452 (49.39)	21953 (51.69)	7929 (52.63)	22129 (50.60)
Fine	18 (0.03)	1 (0.00)	0 (0.00)	7 (0.00)
Interest	665 (1.04)	2134 (5.04)	577 (3.83)	1250 (2.85)
Others	9007 (14.15)	1925 (4.53)	211 (1.40)	4068 (9.29)
Total	63672 (100.0)	42465 (100.0)	15059 (100.0)	43761 (100.0)

Source: Computed from Primary data.
Note: Figures within the parentheses denotes percentages to total.

Savings and bank loan constituted the major proportion of the funds with SHGs (86.55%) followed by interest received on loan and contribution from NGOs. The bank loan constituted the major source funds accounting for 49.39 to 52.63 per cent of the total across different linkage models. Share of NGO contribution was relatively more in model with NGO as intermediary accounting for 7.98 per cent.

Size of Loan

Loans were taken for three purposes. Table 5.6 shows the details of composition of loan portfolio of SHGs during 1998-99.

Table 5.6. Composition of Loan Portfolio of SHGs During 1998-1999

(In Rs.)

Purpose	Models			Overall
	Direct	NGO Facilitator	NGO Interme-diary	
Income Generating Purpose	30192 (65.01)	25858 (63.46)	23804 (91.74)	26938 (68.40)
Non-income Generating Purpose	11127 (23.96)	14137 (34.70)	981 (3.78)	10034 (25.48)
Others	5119 (11.02)	751 (1.84)	1170 (4.51)	2412 (6.12)
Total	46438 (100.00)	40746 (100.00)	25955 (100.00)	39384 (100.00)

Source: Computed from Primary data.
Note: Figures within the parentheses denotes percentages to total.

The average size of loan disbursed by the selected SHGs during the year 2005-2006 was Rs.39,384 of which 68.40 per cent was for income generating purpose and the remaining 31.60 per cent for non-income generating purposes. The size of loan was observed to be relatively more in the groups formed by the banks than the other two models. The share of loans for income generating purpose was significantly higher in NGO intermediary model (91.71%) than NGO facilitator (63.46%) and direct models (65.01%).

Age wise Distribution of Sample Respondents

The data collected from 225 sample swarnagaries are analysed in this part. The profile includes age, community, occupation, level of literacy, activity, etc. The age of the sample beneficiaries of SGSY is presented in Table 5.7.

Table 5.7. Age-wise Distribution of Sample Respondents

Sl. No.	Category	No. of Sample Respondents			Total
		15-30	30-45	45 years & above	
1.	Direct	3	67	5	75
2.	NGO Facilitator	11	42	22	75
3.	NGO Intermediary	12	25	38	75
	Total	26 (11.55)	134 (59.56)	65 (28.89)	225 (100.00)

Source: Computed from Primary data.

Age is another determinant factor which shows the involvement of a particular age group in the SGSY scheme in the district. It is clear from Table 5.7 that most of the sample respondents (59.56%) are in the age group of 30 to 45 years. The 11.55 per cent of the sample are in the age group of 15 to 30 years and the remaining 28.89 per cent are in the age above 45 years. The young women groups are not involved in the SGSY in the study district. The experienced middle age groups (30 to 45 years) help in functioning of SGSY schemes and the SHG approach for rural development.

Community

Table 5.8 shows the details of distribution of sample households.

Table 5.8. Distribution of Sample Households

Community	No. of Sample Respondents	Proportion of Households
Backward Class (BC)	81	36.01
Scheduled Caste (SC)	37	16.44
Scheduled Tribes (ST)	37	16.44
Forward Caste (FC)	70	31.11
Total	225	100.00

Source: Primary data.

The distribution of sample households according to the community revealed that 36.01 per cent of them belonged to the backward class, 32.88 per cent to SC/ST community and 31.11 per cent to the forward caste

Distribution of Sample Households According to Community

Table 5.9 explains the distribution of sample households according to community.

Table 5.9. Distribution of Sample Households according to Community under SHG Models

Community	Model					
	Direct		NGO Facilitator		NGO Intermediary	
	No.	%	No.	%	No.	%
Backward Class (BC)	34	45.33	21	28.00	15	20.00
Scheduled Caste (SC)	17	22.67	17	22.66	13	17.33
Scheduled Tribes (ST)	6	8.00	21	28.00	9	12.00
Forward Caste (FC)	18	24.10	16	21.34	38	50.67
Total	75	100.00	75	100.00	75	100.00

Source: Computed from Primary data.

While backward class dominated the membership in direct and NGOs facilitator model, forward caste members have more representation in NGOs as intermediary model.

Occupation

The distribution of sample households according to main occupation is presented in Table 5.10.

In the sample as a whole agricultural labour constituted around 31.56 per cent followed by small farmers (29.33%) and marginal farmers (23.11%). Other farmers hardly constituted 3.56 per cent of the households.

Table 5.10. Distribution of Sample Households according to Main Occupation

Category*	No. of Sample	Proportion of Member Households (%)
Marginal Farmers (<2.5ha)	52	23.11
Small Farmers (2.5-5.0 ha)	66	29.33
Other Farmers (≥ 5.0 ha)	8	3.56
Agricultural Labourers	71	31.56
Other Occupations	28	12.44
Total	225	100.00

*Some of the farm households are agricultural labourers/ pursuing other occupations.

Source: Computed from Primary data.

Occupational Pattern Under SHG Model

Table 5.11 shows the classification of groups according to SHG models.

Table 5.11. Occupational Pattern under SHG Model

Community	Model					
	Direct		NGO Facilitator		NGO Intermediary	
	No.	%	No.	%	No.	%
Marginal Farmers (≤2.5ha)	17	22.67	28	37.33	22	29.33
Small Farmers (2.5-5.0 ha)	18	24.00	22	29.33	11	14.67
Other Farmers (≥ 5.0 ha)	2	2.67	3	4.00	3	4.00
Agricultural Labourers	27	36.00	11	14.67	34	45.33
Other Occupations	11	14.66	11	14.67	5	6.67
Total	75	100.00	75	100.00	75	100.00

*Some of the farm households are agricultural labourers/ pursuing other occupations.

Source: Computed from Primary data.

The classification of groups according to different models indicated that the participation of agricultural labourers was more in the model with NGOs as intermediary whereas the share of small and marginal farmers was more in the model where banks directly lend to SHGs. The participation of agricultural labourers was higher in the newly formed groups. These trends suggest that SHG experiment is gaining wider acceptance among marginal farmers and agricultural labourers in recent years.

Level of Literacy

The level of literacy of the sample respondents is presented in Table 5.12.

Table 5.12. Distribution of Sample Households according to Literacy

Level of Literacy	No. of Sample	Proportion of Households (%)
Illiterate	54	24.00
Can sign	59	26.22
Primary	47	20.89
Secondary	51	22.67
Higher secondary	12	5.33
Graduate	2	0.89
Total	225	100.00

Source: Computed from Primary data.

About 24.00 per cent of the sample members were illiterate and 26.22 per cent could sign. Members with primary education accounted for 20.89 per cent and those with secondary level constituted 22.67 per cent.

Literacy Model-wise

Table 5.13 shows the Distribution of Sample Households Literacy Model-wise.

Table 5.13. Distribution of Sample Households Literacy Model Wise

Literacy	Model					
	Direct		NGO Facilitator		NGO Intermediary	
	No.	%	No.	%	No.	%
Illiterate	15	20.00	26	34.67	12	16.00
Can sign	23	30.67	20	26.67	16	21.33
Primary	16	21.33	15	20.00	15	20.00
Secondary	17	22.67	11	14.66	25	33.33
Higher secondary	3	4.00	3	4.00	6	8.00
Graduate	1	1.33	-	-	1	1.34
Total	75	100.00	75	100.00	75	100.00

Source: Computed from Primary data.

The classification of groups according to different models indicated that 34.67 per cent in the model with NGOs as facilitator were illiterate. While disaggregating the sample according to the ages of the SHGs, there was a declining trend of illiteracy level from 34.67 per cent to 22 per cent. This indicates that the groups possibly facilitate the members in improving their literacy levels.

Economic Activity

Table 5.14 shows the classification of SHG members according to activities. Non-farm activity constituted the major share accounting for 20.44 per cent, followed by farm activity (17.78%). Though about 32 per cent of the sample households were agricultural labourers, only 14.22 per cent of them depended exclusively on agricultural labour. On the other hand, the remaining 6.67 per cent of them were engaged in other activities in addition to wage earners. About 34.67 per cent of the sample households were engaged in both farm and non-farm (mixed) activities.

Table 5.14. Distribution of Members according to Activities

Activity	No. of Sample	Proportion of Members (%)
Farm activity	40	17.78
Non-farm activity	46	20.44
Agri. labour	32	14.22
Off-farm activity	14	6.22
Mixed	78	34.67
Others	15	6.67
Total	225	100.00

Source: Computed from Primary data.

Economic Activity – Model-wise

Table 5.15 shows the model wise classification of SHG members according to activities.

Table 5.15. Distribution of Sample Households according to Activity – Model-wise

Activity	Model					
	Direct		NGO Facilitator		NGO Intermediary	
	No.	%	No.	%	No.	%
Farm activity	18	24.00	14	18.67	8	10.67
Non-farm activity	19	25.33	10	13.33	16	21.33
Agri. labour	13	17.33	6	8.00	12	16.00
Off-farm activity	4	15.33	5	6.67	6	8.00
Mixed	16	21.34	38	50.67	17	22.67
Others	5	6.67	2	2.66	16	21.33
Total	75	100.00	75	100.00	75	100.00

Source: Computed from Primary data.

Table 5.15 reveals that about 50.67 per cent of the households under model with NGO as facilitator were engaged in mixed activities. This proportion was relatively higher compared to the other two models. Non-farm activity was reported by 25.33 per cent of the members under direct linkage model. The age wise classification of groups indicated that the share of mixed activities showed declining trend as the age of the SHGs progressed.

IMPACT OF MICRO-FINANCE ON SHG MEMBERS

The members of SHGs, it is expected, would have a better access to credit, which they might not have had earlier. Access to credit would bring in its wake economic benefits in terms of increased incomes, higher employment, better living conditions including enhanced consumption levels, etc. In SHGs, access to credit follows the group formation. This is likely to impart a sense of belonging in an individual and may bring about social benefits assertiveness within and outside family circles and other positive behavioural changes before one gets access to credit.

Besides, saving habit is inculcated among the members and part of the lending is accumulated which gives the feeling of self-help and mutual help. Because of these features, the credit management by members of the group is expected to be better. While it is debatable whether economic benefits or the social benefits result first, needless to say, they are mutually reinforcing. In this section, economic benefits accruing to SHG members are discussed covering various parameters such as asset structure, income, savings and borrowing, employment, consumption levels, etc.

Impact on Asset Structure

Value of assets possessed by a household reflects its financial strength and shock absorbing capacity of the household. Thus, increase in the assets held by members is a sign of positive impact. The overall views of the SGSY beneficiaries on the charges in the asset value is given in Table 5.16.

Table 5.16. Changes in Value of Assets due to SHGs

Direction of Change in Assets	No.	Overall (%)
Decreased	10	4.44
No change	83	36.89
Increased	132	58.67
Total	225	100.00

Source: Computed from Primary data.

Viewed from this angle SHG programme is broadly successful as about 58.67 per cent of the sample households reported increase in the assets held by them while 36.89 per cent reported 'no change'. Land, building, milch cattle, work animals, poultry birds, small ruminants like goat and sheep, consumer durables are some of the assets that households maintain. Of these, assets in this study mean assets other than land and buildings. These two forms of assets are excluded for analysis as the changes in them cannot be expected from micro-finance interventions over a short span of time and changes, if any, in these can not, hence, be strictly considered for impact study.

Assets According to Model and Age of SHGs

Table 5.17 shows the assets according to model and age of SHGs.

Table 5.17. Changes in Value of Assets according to Model and Age of SHGs (%)

Direction of Change in Assets	Model					
	Direct		NGO Facilitator		NGO Intermediary	
	No.	%	No.	%	No.	%
Decreased	3	4.00	2	2.67	5	6.67
No change	32	42.57	21	28.00	30	40.00
Increased	40	52.43	52	69.33	40	53.33
Total	75	100.00	75	100.00	75	100.00

Source: Computed from Primary data.

Among different linkage models, the increase in assets was more in model with NGO as facilitator compared to the other two models. The proportion of households reporting increase in the assets showed positive correlation with the age of the groups.

Asset Holding Pattern of Member Households

The average asset value of the SHG member household before and after getting benefits of SGSY is presented in Table 5.18.

Table 5.18. Asset Holding Pattern of Member Households (Rs.)

Type of Asset	Before SGSY		After SGSY	
	Value (Rs.)	Share (%)	Value (Rs.)	Share (%)
Milch cattle	2734	39.98	5221	44.28
Work animals	984	14.38	1122	9.51
Poultry birds	425	6.21	658	5.58
Sub-Total	4143	60.54	7001	59.37
Consumer durables	2700	39.46	4792	40.63
Total	6843	100.00	11793	100.00
Increase in Assets	4950		72.33%	

Source: Computed from Primary data.

An average SHG member household possessed assets worth Rs.11,793 in the reference year compared to Rs.6,843 during pre SGSY benefits period. There was an average increase of 72.3 per cent in the assets held by members after getting the benefits of SGSY.

Asset Holding Pattern of Member Households Model-wise

The average value of assets distributed according to different types of assets in different models are presented in Table 5.19.

Table 5.19. Asset Holding Pattern of Member Households Model-wise (Rs.)

Particulars	Model					
	Direct		NGO Facilitator		NGO Intermediary	
	Before	After	Before	After	Before	After
Milch cattle	2255	4133	4359	7593	1380	3727
Work animals	503	587	1825	1901	576	854
Poultry birds	138	385	656	447	507	1255
Consumer durables	2315	3955	2223	4554	3756	6128
Total	5211	9060	9063	14495	6219	11964
Increase in Assets	3849	73.86	5432	59.93	5745	92.38

Note: Figures in last row under 'before' and 'after' columns are in absolute and % terms, respectively.

Source: Computed from Primary data.

Members of the groups, where NGOs acted as intermediaries, recorded highest increase in the average asset holding to the tune of 92.38 per cent compared to the other two models.

Distribution of Members According to Value of Assets – Overall

Table 5.20 shows the over all distribution of members according to value of assets.

The frequency distribution of the sample households according to the value of assets between pre and post-SGSY situations revealed that there was a shift in the pattern of holding of assets. The above table reveals that about 13.33 per cent of the households were having assets of Rs.15,000 or more in value during pre-SGSY situation.

Increasingly, proportion of households having negligible asset (up to Rs.1000) declined in the post-SHG situation compared to pre-SGSY situation. About one in every three households was having negligible assets in pre-SGSY situation while the frequency declined to one in every six during post-SGSY situation.

Table 5.20. Distribution of Members according to Value of Assets – Overall

Values of Asset (Rs.)	Before		After	
	No.	%	No.	%
Negligible (up to 1000)	79	35.12	36	16.00
1000-2500	24	10.66	19	8.44
2500-5000	27	12.00	26	11.57
5000-7500	23	10.22	28	12.44
7500-10000	18	8.00	28	12.44
10000-15000	24	10.66	32	14.22
≥ 15000	30	13.33	56	24.89
Total	225	100.00	225	100.00

Source: Computed from Primary data.

Impact on Saving and Borrowing Pattern

The concept of micro-finance rests on the premise that members will develop the habit of thrift before they can avail of loans. This, besides increasing the possibility of self-reliance in meeting credit needs of the group members, will help efficiently deploy the credit among the members as their own money is at stake. In this section, the savings pattern of the members is presented followed by the details about their borrowing. The 5.21 shows the average result of savings of the sample households.

From the Table 5.21 it is clear that an average household saved Rs.460 annually before getting the SGSY benefits. During the post-SHG period, the average level of savings increased by more than three times to Rs.1,444. Major agency with which savings were maintained was banks (both co-operatives and commercial banks), in both pre and post-SGSY situation. The savings with banks amounted to Rs.679 followed by Rs.629 with SGSY. Higher increment in savings (85.01 per cent) with the banks indicates the positive impact of the programme on banks as a source of resource mobilization.

Table 5.21. Average Annual Level of Savings of Sample Households

Source	Average level of Savings		
	Before (Rs.)	After (Rs.)	Increment (%)
SHG	—	629	-
Bank	367	679	85.01
Friends	93	136	46.23
Total	460	1444	131.24

Source: Computed from Primary data.

Model-wise Average Annual Level of Savings of Sample

Among different models of linkage, maximum increment in savings was registered in the model with NGO as intermediary. Table 5.22 shows the model-wise average level of saving.

Table 5.22. Model-wise Average Annual Level of Savings of Sample

Agency	Model-wise					
	Direct		NGO Facilitator		NGO Intermediary	
	Before	After	Before	After	Before	After
SHG	-	734	-	676	-	440
Bank	549	911	260	369	267	763
Friends	32	40	165	225	83	148
Total	581	1685	425	1270	350	1351
% change over before		190.02		198.82		286.00

Source: Computed from Primary data.

From Table 5.22, it is clear that however, the average level was the highest in the model where SHGs was directly linked to banks. Under this model, major portion of the savings were maintained with banks.

Average Loan Amount per Member Household

Table 5.23 shows average loan amount per member household.

Table 5.23. Average Loan Amount Per Member Household

Particulars	Loan Amount (Rs.)
Pre-SGSY	4282
Post-SGSY	8341
Increment (%)	94.80

Source: Computed from Primary data.

Any programme dispensing credit normally will aim at 'credit widening' (expanding the clientele base) and 'credit deepening' (enhancing quantum of loans per borrower). The results presented in this section showed that promotion of SHG situation compared to Rs.4,282 in pre-SGSY situation, thus registering an increase of about 94.80 per cent. Out of this, 56 per cent was on account of borrowing by households that were not borrowing in pre SHG situation and the rest was due to increase in the quantum of borrowing per borrowing household.

Average Loan Amount According to Different Categories

Table 5.24 shows the average loan amount borrowed by the member household, category wise.

The level of borrowings increased substantially across different models of linkage, the increase being relatively higher in model with NGO as intermediary.

Table 5.24. Average Loan Amount Borrowed by the Members Households according to Different Categories

	Sl. No.	Category	Average Loan Borrowed		
			Before (Rs.)	After (Rs.)	Increment (%)
Model	1.	Direct	4142	7795	88.19
	2.	NGO Facilitator	4643	9073	95.41
	3.	NGO Intermediary	4048	8192	102.37

Source: Computed from Primary data.

Distribution of Loan Amount According to Agency

Table 5.25 shows the distribution of loan amount according to agency.

Table 5.25. Distribution of Loan Amount according to Agency (%)

Source Agency	Loan Distributed		
	Before	After	Difference
Bank	32.5	20.7	–11.8
FR	15.9	1.0	–14.9
ML	41.6	3.2	–38.4
Others	10.0	0.2	–9.8
SHG	-	74.9	74.9
Total	100.0	100.0	

Source: Computed from Primary data.

The source-wise distribution of amount borrowed by the households showed that SGSY accounted for about 74.90 per cent of the borrowed amount in the post-SGSY situation, while informal agencies like money lenders, friends and relatives, commission agents, etc., accounted for about 67.5 per cent in pre-SGSY situation. The relative importance of banks also came down during the post-SGSY situation i.e., SGSY had substituted the informal agencies to a considerable extent in meeting the credit needs of the members.

Distribution of Borrower Accounts according to Size of Loan

Table 5.26 shows the distribution of borrowers accounts according to size of loan.

Table 5.26. Distribution of Borrower Accounts according to Size of Loan

Loan Size Class (Rs.)	Proportion of Loan Accounts			
	Before		After	
	No.	%	No.	%
Up to 2500	105	46.67	91	40.44
2500-5000	64	28.44	69	30.68
5000-7500	6	2.67	19	8.44
7500-10000	22	9.78	27	12.00
10000-15000	7	3.11	7	3.11
15000-20000	8	3.56	7	3.11
>25000	13	5.78	5	2.22
Total	225	100.00	225	100.00
No. of loan accounts		375.00		900.00
Loan Penetration Ratio		0.67		1.61

Source: Computed from Primary data.

The distribution of borrower accounts according to size of loan showed that 75.11 per cent of the loans were for amounts less than Rs.5000 in pre-SGSY situation compared to 71.12 per cent in the post-SGSY situation. The proportion of loans between Rs.5,000 to Rs.10,000 increased from 12.45 per cent in the pre-SHG period to 20.44 per cent in the post-SGSY situation. Thus, the loan penetration ratio, as measured by number of loan accounts per household, increased considerably from 0.67 to 1.61 under these two situations.

Distribution of Loan Accounts and Amount according to Activity

Table 5.27 shows the distribution of loan accounts and amount borrowed according to activity.

Table 5.27. Distribution of Loan Accounts and Amount according to Activity

Activity	No. of Accounts				Amount (Rs.)	
	Before SGSY		After SGSY		Before	After
	No.	%	No.	%		
Allied to agriculture	14	3.73	165	18.33	3.00	18.30
Consumption	187	49.87	229	25.44	28.30	14.50
Cultivation	102	27.20	209	23.22	24.20	25.80
Investment in agriculture	37	9.87	84	9.33	34.70	15.10
Industries, services & business	30	8.00	183	20.33	6.80	23.10
Miscellaneous	5	1.33	30	3.35	3.00	3.20
Total	375	100.00	900	100.00	100.00	100.00

Source: Computed from Primary data.

Consumption and cultivation were two activities, which accounted for major share (77.07%) of loan accounts in the pre-SGSY situation, accounting for 52.50 per cent of the loan amount. In the post-SGSY situation, share of allied agricultural activities and ISB activities showed increase in the number of accounts as well as amount across all the three models. These activities had 38.66 per cent share in number of accounts and 41.40 per cent in amount borrowed. Thus, there was a shift in the composition of activities due to SGSY.

Distribution of Loan Accounts According to Activity: Model-wise

Table 5.28 shows the distribution of loan accounts according to activity.

Table 5.28. Distribution of Loan Accounts according to Activity: Model-wise

Activity	Model					
	Direct		NGO Facilitator		NGO Intermediary	
	Before	After	Before	After	Before	After
Allied to agriculture	0.0	14.1	3.2	18.0	10.6	24.3
Consumption	46.2	25.5	54.2	24.7	48.0	25.5
Cultivation	29.0	27.5	31.0	26.1	16.0	14.2
Investment	11.0	6.9	7.1	12.0	16.0	8.9
ISB	13.1	22.2	3.9	14.4	6.7	25.9
Miscellaneous	0.7	3.8	0.6	4.8	2.7	1.2
Total	100.0	100.0	100.0	100.0	100.0	100.0

Source: Computed from Primary data.

Model-wise Distribution of Loan Accounts according to Activity

Table 5.29 shows the model-wise distribution of loan accounts according to activity.

Table 5.29. Model-wise Distribution of Loan Accounts according to Activity

Activity	Model					
	Direct		NGO Facilitator		NGO Intermediary	
	Before	After	Before	After	Before	After
Allied to agriculture	0.0	9.3	2.1	22.0	8.1	24.1
Consumption	16.1	13.0	38.3	15.4	29.8	15.1
Cultivation	41.4	33.7	20.5	24.9	7.3	17.6
Investment	30.7	12.3	35.9	18.5	38.4	14.0
ISB	11.7	27.9	3.1	15.3	5.7	27.8
Miscellaneous	0.1	3.8	0.1	3.9	10.7	1.4
Total	100.0	100.0	100.0	100.0	100.0	100.0

Source: Computed from Primary data.

Tables 5.28 and 5.29 reveal that share of consumption loans came down across the models in the total number of loan accounts during the post-SGSY situation. However, the increment in the share of ISB activities was higher in the model with NGO as intermediary.

Agency-wise Distribution of Loan Accounts according to Activity

Tables 5.30 and 5.31 show the agency wise distribution of loan accounts according to activity.

Distribution of loan accounts and amounts according to agencies (Table 5.30 and 5.31) shows that cultivation, ISB and allied agricultural activities were major activities under loans borrowed from banks and account for 42.9 per cent, 35.7 per cent and 15.7 per cent of the accounts and 35.8 per cent, 40.3 per cent and 19.6 per cent of loan amount, during pre and post SGSY situations respectively. Investment on agriculture, allied activities and consumption were the major activities undertaken with amounts borrowed from friends and relatives both in terms of number of loan accounts as well as loan amount. Predominant activities supported by moneylenders were cultivation, consumption, ISB and investment. Almost equal proportion of loan amount was availed for all the activities other than those categorized as 'miscellaneous'.

Interest Rates and Loan Periods

Table 5.32 gives the distribution of borrower accounts and the amount borrowed according to the rate of interest.

There was an unmistakable tendency for the interest rates at which members were borrowing to converge towards 12 to 24 per cent range. About 80.5 per cent of the loan accounts covering 75.6 per cent of the amount were contracted at this rate of interest in post-SGSY situation compared to mere 18 per cent of accounts covering 32.5 per cent of the amount in pre-SGSY situation indicating the

Table 5.30. Agency-wise Distribution of Loan Accounts according to Activity

Activity	Agency									
	Bank		Friends		Money Lenders		SGSY		Others	
	Before	After	Before	After	Before	After	Before	After	Before	After
Allied to agriculture	13.6	15.7	1.9	25.0	0.4	0.0	-	19.0	0.0	0.0
Consumption	6.2	1.4	68.4	25.0	60.4	26.6	-	27.0	61.5	57.1
Cultivation	49.4	42.9	11.1	0.0	23.8	26.7	-	21.9	15.4	0.0
Investment	13.6	4.3	16.7	50.0	7.5	6.7	-	9.6	15.4	14.3
ISB	16.0	35.7	0.0	0.0	7.0	33.3	-	18.8	7.7	28.6
Miscellaneous	1.2	0.0	1.9	0.0	0.9	6.7	-	3.7	0.0	0.0
Total	100.0	100.0	100.0	100.0	100.0	100.0	100.0	100.0	100.0	100.0

Source: Computed from Primary data.

Table 5.31. Agency-wise Distribution of Loan Accounts according to Activity

Activity	Agency									
	Bank		Friends		Money Lenders		SGSY		Others	
	Before	After	Before	After	Before	After	Before	After	Before	After
Allied to agriculture	8.0	19.6	1.8	37.5	0.3	0.0	-	18.7	0.0	0.0
Consumption	5.0	1.0	28.0	20.8	45.8	18.9	-	16.8	31.2	41.4
Cultivation	37.3	35.8	10.8	0.0	24.4	30.3	-	24.0	1.9	0.0
Investment	30.8	3.3	56.8	41.7	21.8	18.6	-	16.9	66.5	20.9
ISB	11.2	41.3	0.0	0.0	7.5	26.0	-	19.9	0.4	37.7
Miscellaneous	7.7	0.0	2.6	0.0	0.2	6.2	-	3.7	0.0	0.0
Total	100.0	100.0	100.0	100.0	100.0	100.0	100.0	100.0	100.0	100.0

Source: Computed from Primary data.

average rural interest rates declined for the SGSY beneficiaries.

Table 5.32. Distribution of Loan Accounts and Amount According to Interest Rate Ranges

Interest Rate (%)	No. of Accounts		Amount (Rs.)	
	Before	After	Before	After
Up to 12	15.1	11.7	15.6	15.0
12-24	17.9	80.5	31.8	75.6
24-36	32.5	6.9	28.8	7.1
36-48	5.3	0.6	6.2	1.1
48-60	22.1	0.3	14.1	1.2
>60	7.0	-	3.5	-
Total	100.0	100.0	100.0	100.0

Source: Computed from Primary data.

Agency-wise Distribution of Loan Accounts

Table 5.33 shows the agency-wise distribution of loan accounts according to activity

Agency-wise distribution of loan accounts reveals that proportion of loan accounts contracted at the rate of interest in the bandwidth of 12 to 24 per cent was maximum under banks loans from friends, moneylenders and other sources were mostly contracted in the range 24 to 36 per cent interest rates. While loans contracted at interest rates in the range of 48 to 60 per cent were insignificant in proportion, no loans were taken at interest rates above 60 per cent in post-SGSY situation.

Agency-wise Distribution of Loan Amounts

Table 5.34 shows the agency-wise distribution of loan amounts according to activity.

Table 5.33. Agency-wise Distribution of Loan Accounts according to Activity (%)

Interest Rate	Agency									
	Bank		Friends		Moneylenders		SGSY		Others	
	Before	After	Before	After	Before	After	Before	After	Before	After
Up to 12	62.8	33.3	0.0	25.0	2.2	0.0	-	10.2	0.0	0.0
12-24	37.2	66.7	6.8	0.0	13.0	6.7	-	83.8	25.0	28.6
24-36	0.0	0.0	65.9	50.0	35.9	73.3	-	5.5	58.4	71.4
36-48	0.0	0.0	2.3	0.0	7.6	6.7	-	0.5	8.3	0.0
48-60	0.0	0.0	25.0	25.0	30.5	13.3	-	0.0	0.0	0.0
>60	0.0	-	-	-	10.8	-	-	-	8.3	-
Total	100.0	100.0	100.0	100.0	100.0	100.0	100.0	100.0	100.0	100.0

Source: Computed from Primary data.

Table 5.34. Agency-wise Distribution of Loan Amounts according to Activity (%)

Interest Rate	Agency									
	Bank		Friends		Moneylenders		SGSY		Others	
	Before	After	Before	After	Before	After	Before	After	Before	After
Up to 12	44.3	38.0	0.0	37.5	2.8	0.0	-	11.1	0.0	0.0
12-24	55.7	62.0	9.6	0.0	13.6	3.1	-	82.4	63.2	33.5
24-36	0.0	0.0	85.2	41.7	36.1	44.3	-	6.2	7.5	66.5
36-48	0.0	0.0	0.3	0.0	8.5	24.8	-	0.3	25.1	0.0
48-60	0.0	0.0	4.9	20.8	31.7	27.9	-	0.0	0.0	0.0
>60	0.0	0.0	0.0	0.0	7.3	0.0	-	0.0	4.2	0.0
Total	100.0	100.0	100.0	100.0	100.0	100.0	100.0	100.0	100.0	100.0

Source: Computed from Primary data.

Distribution of Loan Accounts and Amount According to Interest Rate Ranges

Table 5.35 shows the distribution of loan accounts and amount according to interest rate ranges.

Table 5.35. Distribution of Loan Accounts and Amount according to Interest Rate Ranges (%)

Interest Rate (%)	No. of Accounts		Amount (Rs.)	
	Before	After	Before	After
Up to 3	13.7	4.8	3.6	1.7
6-6	20.6	14.2	14.3	12.5
6-12	46.4	57.8	39.9	52.3
12-24	4.8	13.1	6.9	16.4
24-36	4.6	7.9	10.1	13.1
>36	9.9	2.2	25.2	4.0
Total	100.0	100.0	100.0	100.0

Source: Computed from Primary data.

Most of the loans contracted were for a period of less than 12 months both in terms of number of accounts and amount. There was a tendency to converge towards 6 to 12 month period. Term loans of more than 36 months duration, which accounted for one-fourth of the loan amount in pre-SHG period, accounted for only 4 per cent in the post-SHG period.

Agency wise Distribution of Loan Accounts According to Loan Period

Tables 5.36 and 5.37 show the agency wise distribution of loan accounts according to loan period and according to activity.

Terms of loans of more than 36 months duration were less preferred in post-SGSY period, compared to the earlier times as indicated by the decline in their share. Their share

Table 5.36. Agency-wise Distribution of Loan Accounts according to Loan Period

Interest Rate	Agency									
	Bank		Friends		Moneylenders		SGSY		Others	
	Before	After	Before	After	Before	After	Before	After	Before	After
Up to 3	0.0	1.4	7.4	0.0	20.7	0.0	-	5.1	0.0	14.3
6-6	1.3	8.6	24.0	25.0	27.3	40.0	-	14.2	7.7	0.0
6-12	49.4	40.0	51.9	75.0	42.3	26.6	-	59.8	76.9	71.4
12-24	6.3	5.7	11.1	0.0	3.1	6.7	-	13.9	0.0	14.3
24-36	10.1	23.9	5.6	0.0	2.6	6.7	-	5.9	0.0	0.0
>36	32.9	11.4	0.0	0.0	4.0	20.0	-	1.1	15.4	0.0
Total	100.0	100.0	100.0	100.0	100.0	100.0	100.0	100.0	100.0	100.0

Source: Computed from Primary data.

Table 5.37. Agency-wise Distribution of Loan Accounts according to Activity (%)

Interest Rate	Agency									
	Bank		Friends		Moneylenders		SGSY		Others	
	Before	After	Before	After	Before	After	Before	After	Before	After
Up to 3	0.0	0.1	1.9	0.0	7.8	0.0	-	2.0	0.0	9.2
6-6	2.2	6.2	23.6	37.5	21.9	42.7	-	12.2	4.2	0.0
6-12	30.4	33.5	40.7	62.5	44.2	27.6	-	56.8	50.2	78.2
12-24	9.6	6.3	11.4	0.0	4.7	6.8	-	19.0	0.0	12.6
24-36	5.6	35.7	22.4	0.0	11.1	18.6	-	8.7	0.0	0.0
>36	52.2	18.2	0.0	0.0	10.3	4.3	-	1.3	45.6	0.0
Total	100.0	100.0	100.0	100.0	100.0	100.0	100.0	100.0	100.0	100.0

Source: Computed from Primary data.

in number and amount of loans declined from 32.9 and 51.9 per cent, respectively, in pre-SGSY period to 11.1 and 18.6 per cent, in the same order, in the post-SGSY period.

Repayment Pattern

Table 5.38 shows the agency wise repayment percentage of member household.

Table 5.38. Agency-wise Repayment Percentage of Member Household (%)

Agency	Repayment Percentage		
	Before	After	Increment (% Points)
Banks	63.3	92.4	29.1
Friends & Relatives	90.0	89.6	-0.4
Moneylenders	95.3	82.7	-12.6
SHGs	-	94.4	94.4
Others	94.7	93.6	-1.1
Overall	83.9	93.6	9.7

Source: Computed from Primary data.

The repayment percentage among the sample households from all the sources was 93.6 per cent in post-SGSY situation registering an increase of 9.7 per cent compared to the pre-SGS situation. In general, there was not much improvement in the repayment percentage as it was already at a higher level in pre-SGSY period, the significant improvement in the repayment percentage of bank loans of the order of 29.1 per cent points notwithstanding.

The pre-SGSY recovery might be higher on account of two reasons. First, households were mostly dependent on informal sources such as moneylenders for their credit needs in the pre-SGSY situation. They were availing of loans at higher rates of interest for shorter period of less than 12 months. The informal agencies would be recovering their loans unscrupulously and borrowers also would be giving priority to repayment of these loans as they carry higher rates of interest and as it would ensure loans in future. Second, there is a likelihood of groups comprising people with good recovery ethics, as non-repayment of earlier loans was a barrier to entry in some of the SGSY.

Repayment Percentage of Member Households

Table 5.39 shows the repayment percentage of member households.

Table 5.39. Repayment Percentage of Member Households (%)

Sl.No.	Category	Before	After	Increment
1.	Direct	83.5	97.8	14.3
2.	NGO Facilitator	88.8	93.6	5.6
3.	NGO Intermediary	78.9	88.7	9.8

Source: Computed from Primary data.

The repayment percentage improved under all the three linkage models in the post-SGSY situation, although it was better in model with direct linkage with banks and lowest in the model with NGO as intermediary. Older groups showed higher recovery compared to the younger ones.

Income Generation

Income of the households is one of the important parameters reckoned in any evaluation programme of economic development to assess the success. In this section, besides discussing the income levels in pre and post-SGSY situations, proportion of households who could cross poverty line between these periods also is estimated and presented. Table 5.40 shows the average net income of households per annum according to different categories.

Table 5.40. Average Net Income of Households Per Annum according to Different Categories

Sl. No.	Category	Before (Rs.)	After (Rs.)	Incremental Income (Rs.)	% as Increase
1.	Direct	19604	25834	6230	31.78
2.	NGO Facilitator	18484	25018	6534	35.34
3.	NGO Intermediary	22980	30525	7545	32.83

Source: Computed from Primary data.

The average income in pre- and post-SGSY situations worked out to Rs. 20,356 and Rs. 27,126 respectively. The increase in the net income was to the tune of Rs.6770 i.e., 33.25 per cent of the pre-SGSY situation. Model with NGO as financial intermediary has registered maximum impact in absolute terms with an incremental income of Rs.7545 although in terms of percentage increases, model with NGOs as facilitator registered the highest increase of 32.83 per cent.

Distribution of Households According to Average Net income per Annum

Table 5.41 shows the distribution of households according to average net income per annum.

Table 5.41. Distribution of Households according to Average Net Income Per Annum

Income Range (Rs.)	Before		After	
Up to 7500	17.8	3.7	6.8	1.3
7500-15000	36.0	21.5	22.1	10.1
15000-22500	20.1	18.6	28.1	19.6
Sub Total	73.9	43.8	57.0	31.0
22500-30000	11.0	14.5	15.7	15.7
30000-37500	4.3	7.5	9.4	11.8
37500-45000	3.1	6.3	4.9	7.4
45000-52500	2.2	5.3	3.6	6.6
>52500	5.5	22.6	9.4	27.5

Source: Computed from Primary data.

Table 5.41 gives distribution of households according to the annual average income. In the pre-SGSY period about 36 per cent of the households were having income in the range of Rs. 7,500 - Rs.15,000 followed by 20.1 per cent of the households in the range of Rs. 15,000 - Rs. 22,500. About 73.9 per cent of the households were having an income less than Rs. 22,500. In post-SGSY period, this proportion declined to 57 per cent indicating shift in the income distribution to higher slabs. Similar trend was observed in average loan amount also.

Distribution of Activities and Incremental Income according to Activity Type

Table 5.42 shows the distribution of activities and incremental income according to activity type.

Table 5.42. Distribution of Activities and Incremental Income according to Activity Type (%)

Type of Activity	Before	After	Increment Income
Agri. Labour	26.6	22.7	–3.9
Farm activity	38.7	34.5	–4.2
NFS	23.0	26.1	3.1
Off-farm activity	8.6	13.6	5.6
Other	3.1	3.1	0.0
Total	100.0	100.0	100.0
No. of activities	1114	1314	
Average No. of activities	2.11	2.36	
Per HH			

Source: Computed from Primary data.

The sample households had been undertaking a host of activities that were classified under. Agricultural labour, farm activity, non-farm activity, off-farm activity and others (includes salaries, pension etc.) in the post-SGSY situation about 1,314 activities are taken up by the sample households compared to 1,114 taken up during pre-SGSY situation. Thus, each member household has taken up 2.11 and 2.36 activities in pre and post-SGSY situations, respectively.

Model wise Distribution of Incremental Income According to Activity

Table 5.43 shows the model wise distribution of incremental income according to activity.

Table 5.43. Model Wise Distribution of Incremental Income according to Activity

Type of Activity	Model		
	Direct	NGO Facilitator	NGO Intermediary
Agri. Labour	4.3	4.0	4.1
Farm activity	29.6	23.6	31.5
NFS	53.3	35.6	38.5
Off-farm activity	12.8	27.4	22.7
Other	0.0	9.4	3.2
Total	100.0	100.0	100.0

Source: Computed from Primary data.

About 42.46 per cent of the incremental income generated was from NFS activities followed by farm (28.23 per cent) and off-farm (20.96 per cent) activities. Across all the models of linkage share of NFS activities was higher compared to other activities.

Employment Generation

Easy access to credit provides opportunities for undertaking income-generating activities as a result of which the employment opportunities at the household level increases. Table 5.44 shows the employment per household among different categories of activities during pre and post-SGSY situation.

Table 5.44. Employment Per Household among Different Categories of Activities During Pre and Post-SGSY Situation

Activity	Employment Generated		
	Before	After	Incremental Employment
Farm activity	167 (52.19)	176 (46.93)	9 (5.4)
Non-farm activity	103 (32.19)	130 (34.66)	27 (26.2)
Off-farm activity	50 (15.62)	69 (18.41)	19 (38.0)
Total	320 (100.00)	375 (100.00)	55 (17.2)

Note: Figures in brackets are percentages to total.
Source: Computed from Primary data.

The employment per household during pre-SHG situation was 320 persons, which increased to 375 during post-SHG situation. The estimated incremental employment was 55 persons (17.2%) between pre and post-SGSY situation. While 52.19 per cent of the employment generated was from farm activities during pre-SGSY situation, it was only 46.93 per cent during post-SGSY situation. On the other hand, the proportion of employment generated through non-farm and off-farm activities increased from 32.19 per cent and 15.62 per cent during pre-SGSY situation to 34.66 per cent and 18.41 per cent during post-SGSY situation, respectively.

Model wise Incremental Employment Between Pre and Post-SGSY Situation

Table 5.45 shows the model wise incremental employment between pre and post-SGSY situation.

Table 5.45. Model-wise Incremental Employment between Pre and Post-SGSY Situation

Activity	Direct	NGO Facilitator	NGO Intermediary
Farm activity	5 (5.6)	13 (8.9)	4 (2.0)
Non-farm activity	21 (25.6)	23 (26.4)	43 (28.6)
Off-farm activity	11 (17.7)	32 (51.6)	15 (75.0)
Total	41 (13.4)	68 (23.1)	61 (16.7)

Note: Figures in brackets are percentages to total.
Source: Computed from Primary data.

The impact of micro-finance on employment was relatively higher in NGO facilitating model (23 per cent), followed by NGO intermediary model (17 per cent) and direct model (13 per cent).

Consumption Pattern

Participation of households in the SHG-Bank linkage programme significantly contributed to the increase in their income and thereby their level of living. One of the important indicators of the level of living being consumption levels, in this section, consumption level and its pattern in pre and post-SGSY periods are discussed. Table 5.46 shows the item wise distribution of consumption expenditure during pre and post-SHG situations

The consumption expenditure per month per household was Rs.799 during pre-SGSY situation and registered 24.3 per cent increase to reach to Rs.993 in post-SHG situation. In terms of per capita consumption also similar trend was observed and per capita consumption rose from Rs.197 to Rs. 249 between pre and post-SGSY situation.

Table 5.46. Item -wise Distribution of Consumption Expenditure during Pre and Post-SHG Situations

Item	Per Capita Consumption (Rs.)		Consumption (%)	
	Before	After	Before	After
Food	117	140	60.1	57.1
Clothing	23	31	11.5	12.5
Education	13	20	6.1	7.5
Health	14	20	6.7	7.4
Festivals/ recreation	21	29	10.4	11.2
Others	9	10	5.1	4.3
Total	197	249	100.0	100.0
Consumption (Rs.) / month per household change between pre & post SGSY	799	993		24.3

Source: Computed from Primary data.

The expenditure on food accounted for 60.1 per cent during pre-SGY situation followed by clothing and festival/ creation. Similar trend was observed during post-SGSY situation. However, the expenditure on food came down to 57.1 per cent. The per capita expenditure on food had increased from Rs.117 to Rs.140 accounting for 20 per cent increase between pre and post-SGSY situation. Similarly, the expenditure on clothing, education, health and festivals etc., had registered an increase in the post-SGSY situation.

Distribution of Consumption Expenditure

Tables 5.47 and 5.48 shows the distribution of consumption expenditure during pre and post-SHGS situations among different models.

Table 5.47. Distribution of Consumption Expenditure during Pre and Post-SHG Situations among Different Models

Item	Model					
	Direct		NGO Facilitator		NGO Intermediary	
	Before	After	Before	After	Before	After
Consumption Expenditure (Rs./ month)	757	944	867	1078	750	931
Per capita Expenditure (Rs./ month)	195	243	198	246	210	261
Change between pre & post SGSY periods	24.7	—	24.33	—	24.3	—

Source: Computed from Primary data.

From the Table 5.47 it is clear that the per capita expenditure had increased from Rs.195 to Rs.243 in Direct model, Rs.198 to Rs.246 in NGO Facilitator model and Rs.210 to Rs.261 in NGO Intermediary model.

Table 5.48. Distribution of Consumption Expenditure during Pre and Post-SHG Situations among Different Models

Item	Model					
	Direct		NGO Facilitator		NGO Intermediary	
	Before	After	Before	After	Before	After
Food	64.5	60.3	56.7	54.0	60.2	58.4
Clothing	10.3	11.5	12.7	14.3	11.1	10.6
Education	6.3	8.1	4.4	6.1	8.8	9.2
Health	6.3	6.8	6.8	7.5	7.1	8.0
Festivals/ recreation	10.0	11.1	11.9	12.2	8.4	9.4
Others	2.6	2.2	7.5	5.9	4.4	4.4
Total	100.0	100.0	100.00	100.0	100.0	100.0

Source: Computed from Primary data.

Among different models, there were no significant differences in the increase in the monthly consumption expenditure per household between pre and post-SGSY situation.

Training Input to Members

Training is a very important input, especially in the context of low level of literacy and poor skills. SGSY beneficiaries were being trained by various agencies on a whole range of activities including *Agarbatti* making, tailoring, carpentry and management related aspects such as leadership, book keeping etc. The topics were classified into broad categories related to agriculture, NFS, management and educational topics.

Training Status

Table 5.49 shows the category-wise proportion of members who received training.

Table 5.49. Category-wise Proportion of Members who Received Training

Model	Number	Proportion (%)
Direct	23	29.62
NGO Facilitator	26	35.19
NGO Intermediary	26	35.19
Overall	75	100.00

Source: Computed from Primary data.

Among different models, the training coverage of members was higher in model with NGO involvement (35.19% to 29.62%) compared to the direct linkage model. The differences in the proportion of trained members partly explain the differential economic and social impact across linkage models.

Training Agencies

Table 5.50 shows the category-wise distribution of members who received training.

Table 5.50. Category Wise Distribution of Members who Received Training

Item	Model						
	Direct		NGO Facilitator		NGO Intermediary		Overall
	No.	%	No.	%	No.	%	
Banks	12	16.00	2	2.67	5	6.67	8.46
Govt. Agencies	7	9.34	15	20.00	16	21.33	16.88
NGO	56	74.66	58	77.33	54	72.00	74.66
Total	75	100.00	75	100.00	75	100.00	100.00

Source: Computed from Primary data.

Banks, Government agencies and NGOs are important agencies that impart training to members. NGOs arrange training, in many situations, through private parties and local resource persons. NGOs train three-fourths of the trained members. Government agencies and banks impart training to 16.00 to 8.46 per cent of the trained members. In the models with involvement of NGOs, about one-fifth of the trained members received training from government agencies and three-fourths received from NGOs.

Topics of Training

Table 5.51 shows the proportion of members who received training – Category-wise.

Table 5.51. Proportion of Members who received Training – Categorise-wise

Item	Model							
	Direct		NGO Facilitator		NGO Intermediary		Overall	
	No.	%	No.	%	No.	%		
Agriculture	5	6.67	9	12.00	2	2.67	5	6.67
Educational	-	0.00	3	4.00	2	2.67	2	2.67
Management	15	20.00	35	46.67	27	36.00	26	36.00
NFS	55	73.33	28	37.33	44	58.66	42	54.66
Total	75	100.00	75	100.00	75	100.00	75	100.00

Source: Computed from Primary data.

Training was imparted on a variety of topics. On the whole, Non-Farm Sectors (NFS) related topics dominated with coverage of about 54.66 per cent of the trained members. Next importance was topics related to management aspects. NFS topics dominated in direct linkage model while all topics were given some importance or other in other two models.

Utility of Training

Table 5.52 shows the agency wise opinion of members on the usefulness of the training.

Table 5.52. Agency Wise Opinion of Members on the Usefulness of the Training Received

Agency	Model							
	Direct		NGO Facilitator		NGO Intermediary		Overall	
	No.	%	No.	%	No.	%		
Not useful	50	22.22	20	8.88	7	3.12	13	5.77
Somewhat useful	50	22.22	78	34.67	41	18.22	48	21.34
Useful	75	33.34	88	39.12	115	51.11	107	47.56
Very useful	50	22.22	39	17.33	62	27.55	57	25.33
Total	225	100.00	225	100.00	225	100.00	225	100.00

Source: Computed from Primary data.

Members' opinion about the usefulness of the training given to them revealed that less than 5.77 per cent of the members trained felt that the training was not useful. The remaining members experienced different degrees of utility of the training with one-fourth with 94.33 per cent of them finding it useful and very useful.

Utility of SGSY

The SGSY programme aims to provide credit plus related services and also focus on empowerment of the SHG members with emphasis on women. However, the perceptions and expectations of the people who joined the SGSY programme may be quite different. It is important to know, for the purpose of reconciling the programme objectives and expectations of the people, the perceptions of the people. In this section, the opinion of the SGSY beneficiaries on the utility of SGSY is presented. Table 5.53 shows the proportion of members expressing the opinion on the utility of the groups.

Table 5.53. Proportion of Members Expressing the Opinion on the Utility of the Groups

Opinion	No. of Sample Beneficiaries	Overall
Source of consumption loan	21	48
Source of production loan	15	33
Link to get loan from banks	20	46
Agency to solve social and community problems	15	33
Elevates social status	16	35
Link to other agencies of government	13	30
Total	100	225

Source: Computed from Primary data.

It was found that about 90 per cent members visualized SHGs as a source of credit, especially for consumption loans and also as liaison between them and the banks to get loans. Still 65 per cent of them consider SGSY helpful in solving social and community problems, as they reported that the involvement with SHGs increased their social status. However, about 60 per cent of the members expressed that the groups acted as intermediary/link to other agencies of the government. About 65 per cent of them opined that the groups provided scope for capital formation within the household.

Lower portion of members from older groups viewed SHGs as a source of consumption loan. However, in respect of all other opinions i.e. about the group as an agent to solve social problems, as a means of elevating social status, as a link with other agencies and helpful in capital formation, proportion of members agreeing was higher in older groups.

Table 5.54. Model-wise Proportion of Members Expressing the Opinion on the Utility of the SGSY

Item	Model					
	Direct		NGO Facilitator		NGO Intermediary	
	No.	%	No.	%	No.	%
Source of consumption loan	18	24.00	15	20.00	15	20.00
Source of production loan	13	17.33	10	13.33	10	13.34
Link to get loan from banks	14	18.66	17	21.33	15	20.00
Agency to solve social and community problems	8	10.66	12	16.00	14	18.67
Elevates social status	12	16.01	12	16.00	11	14.66
Link to other agencies of government	10	13.34	10	13.34	10	13.33
Total	75	100.00	75	100.00	75	100.00

Source: Computed from Primary data.

It is expected that members under the models with involvement of NGOs may view SHGs in a broader perspective compared to those under model with direct linkage because of their higher degree of interaction with NGO workers. The results of the model-wise analysis broadly confronted to this a priori reasoning. Relatively higher proportion of members (24%) (Table 5.54) under direct linkage model viewed SHGs as a source of loan compared to the other two models. Similarly, higher proportion of members under this model also felt that SHGs were helpful in capital formation. In respect of opinion on other aspects, i.e., about the group as an agent to solve social problems, as a means of elevating social status, as a link with other agencies and with banks, members of groups under models involving NGOs showed agreement more frequently compared to direct linkage model.

DATA ANALYSIS

Inequality in Savings Pattern

The collected primary data have been analysed with suitable statistical tools in the present section. The statistical tools are: Lorenz curve, multiple regression, correlation coefficient etc. Table 5.55 shows the distribution of cumulative savings according to deciles.

Table 5.55. Distribution of Cumulative Savings according to Deciles

Decile	Pre-SGSY	Post-SGSY
1.	0.0	1.9
2.	0.0	6.2
3.	0.0	6.2
4.	0.0	10.5
5.	0.0	13.6
6.	0.0	17.0
7.	0.0	26.1
8.	0.7	34.6
9.	20.7	51.6
10.	100.0	100.0

Source: Computed from Primary data.

Data show that in pre-SGSY situation about 80 per cent of the savings were made by top 10 per cent of the households. In fact, only 23 per cent of the households reported savings during this period. In post-SGSY situation, the tendency has

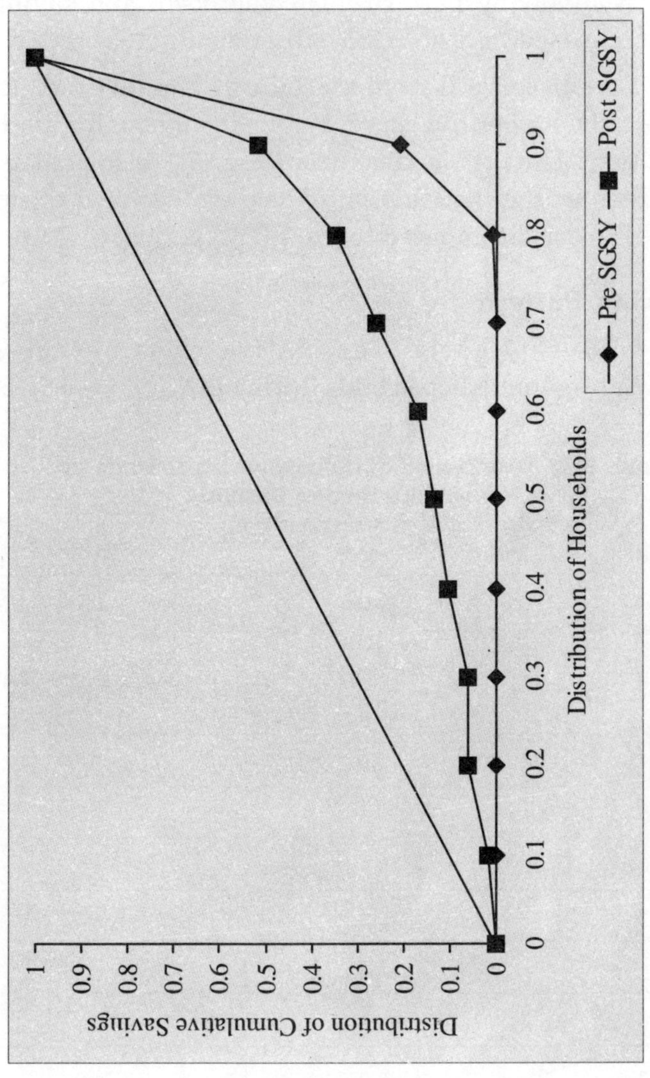

Fig. 5.1. Lorenz Curve showing Distribution of Cumulative Savings according to Deciles

changed and bottom 70 per cent of households accounted for 26 per cent of the savings and the share of top ten per cent households came down to about 49 per cent. Thus, the inequality in saving pattern has come down and savings were broad based in post-SGSY situation.

The Lorenz curve is from the Line of Equality (i.e., the diagonal), the higher the curve, higher the inequality in the distribution. Thus, it is clear from Fig. 5.1 also that the inequalities in the distribution of savings declined during post-SGSY period compared to pre-SGSY period.

Borrowing Pattern

Table 5.56 shows the cumulative distribution of borrowing by sample households during pre and post-SGSY periods.

Table 5.56. Distribution of Cumulative Borrowings by Households among Deciles

Decile	Pre-SGSY	Post-SGSY
1.	0.0	0.2
2.	0.0	2.9
3.	0.0	6.2
4.	0.0	10.0
5.	2.4	15.0
6.	7.4	20.3
7.	12.3	30.2
8.	24.9	43.9
9.	39.7	63.1
10.	100.0	100.0

Source: Computed from Primary data.

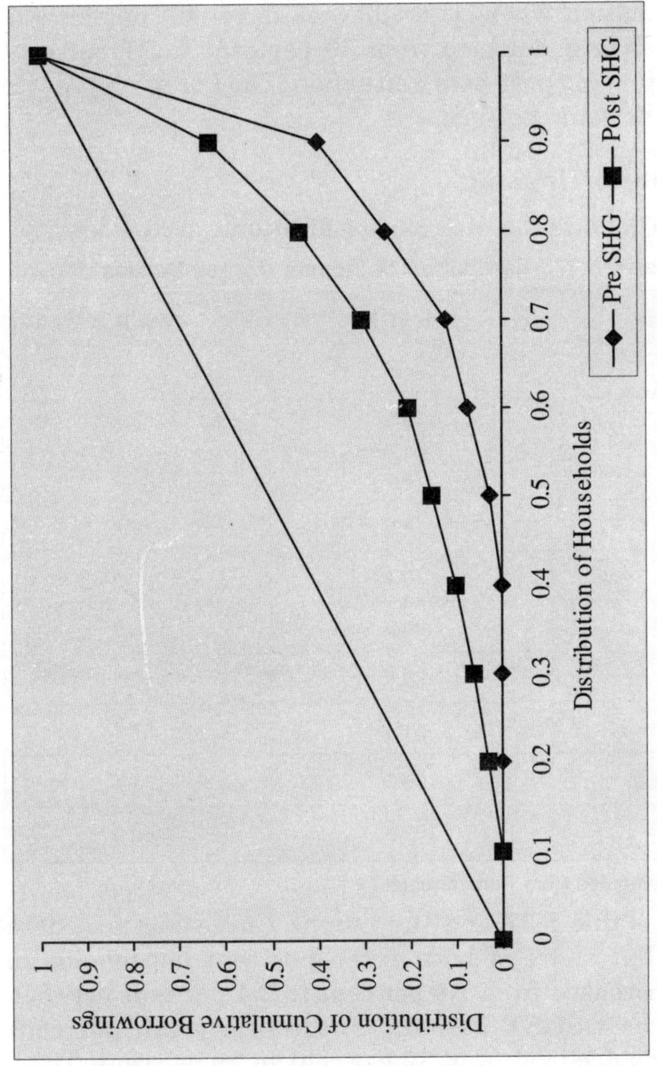

Fig. 5.2. Lorenz Curve showing Distribution of Cumulative Borrowings by Households among Deciles

From Table 5.56 and the Lorenz Curve Fig. 5.2 it is clear that bottom 40 per cent of the households could corner 10 per cent of the credit in post-SHG situation compared to pre-SGSY situation when no credit was flowing. The share of top 10 per cent declined from 60 per cent to 37 per cent between pre and post-SGSY situation. The Lorenz curve also showed the same pattern.

Inequality of Income

Table 5.57 shows the distribution of income across deciles.

Table 5.57. Distribution of Income Across Deciles

Decile	Pre-SGSY	Post-SGSY
1.	1.4	2.4
2.	4.7	6.8
3.	9.8	12.0
4.	16.5	19.4
5.	22.4	25.4
6.	30.3	33.9
7.	39.8	43.5
8.	51.4	57.7
9.	68.0	71.1
10.	100.0	100.0

Source : Computed from Primary data.

From Table 5.57 and the Lorenz Curve Fig. 5.3, data reveals that share of bottom ten per cent households in income increased from 1.4 per cent to 2.4 per cent between pre and post-SGSY periods. Share of top ten per cent households declined from 32 per cent to 29 per cent. Thus, the distribution of income is relatively less unequal in post-SGSY period. This indicates that micro-finance, besides facilitating an increase in the income of the member

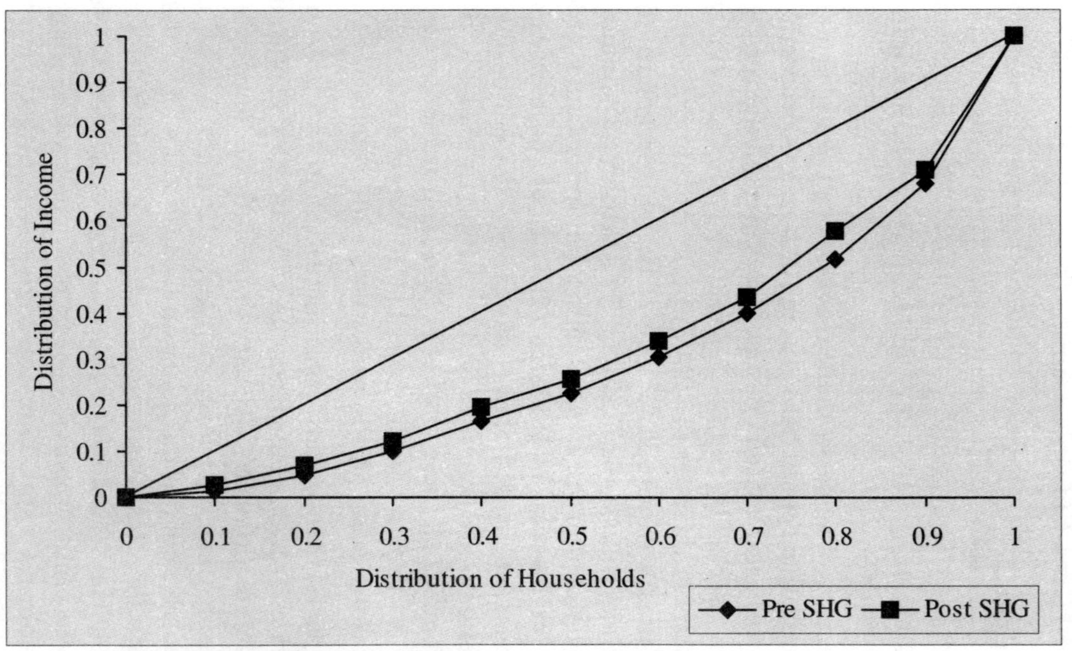

Fig. 5.3. Lorenz Curve showing Distribution of Income across Deciles

households, also helps in reducing the inequalities in the levels of income between the members households.

Traits of Micro-Entrepreneurs

Primary data were collected from the micro-enterprises of the 45 SHGs units in Kanyakumari district. The collected data has been analysed in this section. The managerial performance is measured in order to identify the traits of the entrepreneurs.

The managerial performance is measured in terms of (*i*) rate of output; (*ii*) credit rate; (*iii*) profit rate and proportion of net profit reinvested. It also examines the extent of variations exerted by the 20 explanatory variables namely: (1) Capital intensity-I (2) Capital intensity-II (3) Entrepreneur's education (4) Age of the entrepreneurs (5) Previous experience (6) Training (7) Ancestry (8) Dummy for proprietorship firm (9) Dummy for inheritance (10) Dummy for location of the firm (11) Age of the firm (12) Compensation ratio (13) Market extension (14) Entrepreneurial Behaviour Index (EBI) (15) Sales[1] (16) Institutional credit support[2] (17) Non-institutional credit support (18) Dummy for family type (19) Parent's education and (20) Emigration on the performance indicators.

The performance indicators identified in the present study reflects various entrepreneurial traits. Rate of output indicates entrepreneur's capacity to produce the maximum output from the given level of inputs. In other words, it reflects entrepreneurs' efficiency on the utilization of inputs. Credit rate shows his repaying capacity. Profit rate indicates his managerial talent in the utilization of operating assets to generate profit proportion of net profit reinvested shows entrepreneur's aspiration for higher earning through modernization and expansion.

The arithmetic mean of the performance indicator of SHG units is given in Table 5.58.

Table 5.58. Arithmetic Mean of the Performance Indicator

Sl. No.	Indicators	Mean Value
1.	Rate of output	1.91
2.	Credit rate (in percent)	9.92
3.	Profit rate (in percent)	19.03
4.	Proportion of net reinvested (in percent)	19.95

Source: Computed from Primary data.
Note: The credit rates of only those who have availed themselves of long term loans have been considered for the calculation of the average credit rate.

Separate multiple linear regression equations have been estimated to assess the nature of the influence and the extent of variations exerted by the explanatory variables on the performance indicators, using Ordinary Least Squares (OLS) method. Zero order correlation coefficient has been computed to examine the presence of high multi co linearity among the explanatory variables. Simple correlation coefficient is considered high if it is greater than or equal to 0.8 following Heady and Dillon.[3]

Rate of Output

All the 16 explanatory variables taken together have accounted for 87.6 per cent of variations in the rate of output. In the estimated multiple linear regression equation for micro-enterprise model, five variables have statistically significant co-efficient.

Ancestry and entrepreneur's education appear to be the most important variables influencing positively the rate of output in the model. The positive and significant co-efficient of the two variables suggest that an entrepreneur could produce more output from the given inputs utilizing the knowledge he has gained through his education, specifically technical and professional qualification, and his family business background. The variable 'compensation ratio' has positive and significant coefficient. A unit increase in the

Table 5.59. Estimated Values of Coefficients in the Multiple Linear Regression Equation Fitted for Micro-Enterprise

Sl. No.	Explanatory Variable	Dependent Variable			
		Output Rate	Credit Rate	Profit Rate	Reinvest-ment Rate
1.	Capital Intensity – I	0.090*	(-) 0.00132 (-1.124)	0.0031 (1/024)	0.0057* (3.685)
2.	Capital intensity – II	0.061 (1.281)	(-) 0.0018 (-0.1412)	(-) 0.0005 (-0.095)	(-) 0.005 (-0.095)
3.	Entrepreneur's Education	0.2518** (1.198)	(-) 0.0091 (-0.1412)	0.236** (2.2125)	0.162** (1.36)
4.	Age of the entrepreneur	0.0125 (1.031)	(-) 0.000721 (-1.053)	0.0274 (1.724)	(-) 0.0042 (-072)
5.	Previous experience	(-) 0.0017 (0.601)	(-) 0.015 (1.2134)	0.042 (1.72)	0.0148 (0.652)
6.	Training	(-) 0.0034 (-0.702)	0.0062 (0.2421)	(-) 0.007 (-1.213)	0.0001 (0.021)
7.	Ancestry	0.3479* (2878)	0.0521 (0.614)	0.3132 (1.75)	0.2812* (3.26)
8.	Dummy for Proprietorship	0.352 (0.121)	(-) 0.4021 (-2.708)	(-) 0.112 (-0.029)	0.2418 (1.10)
9.	Dummy for inheritance	0.0421 (0.139)	(-) 0.4241 (-3.05)	(-) 0.189 (-0.565)	0.0384 (0.182)

10.	Dummy for location of the firm	(–)0.0089 (–0.037)	0.1075 (0.342)	0.531 (1.72)	0.1140 (0.619)
11.	Age of the firm	(–) 0.0212 (–1.279)	0.0212* (2.736)	0.030 (1.492)	(–) 0.0040 (–0.318)
12.	Compensation ratio	0.0284* (3.421)	(–) 0.0057 (–1.486)	(–) 0.00330** (2.21)	0.0185* (3.216)
13.	Market extension	(–) 0.2021 (–1.051)	(–) 0.0642 (–0.0398)	0.621 (0.152)	1.704 (0.778)
14.	Entrepreneurial Behaviour Index	(–) 0.7219 (–0.241)	(–) 0.0642 (–0.0398)	0.621 (0.152)	1.704 (0.778)
15.	Institutional Credit Support	0.0021 (0.402)	-	0.0121** (–2.24)	0.0101** (2.20)
16.	Non-Institutional Credit Support	(–) 0.0424* (–3.265)	-	(–) 0.4026* (–2.65)	(–0.0221**) (–2.237)
17.	Sales	-	0.00003 (0.5975)	0.0001 (0.907)	0.00007 (0.165)
	Constant	–2.345** (–2.295)	1.164* (2.405)	(–) 4.174* (–2.659)	(–) 1.402 (–2.2421)
	R^2 value	0.876	0.526	0.912	0.945
	F value	21.07*	3.42	26.011*	50.27*

*Indicates 1 per cent level of significance.
**Indicates 5 per cent level of significance.

wages of skilled workers in relation to the total wages has resulted in 0.028 unit increase in the rate of output.

The coefficient of capital intensity-I has been positive and significant. It suggests that a unit increase in the fixed capital labour ratio has raised the rate of output by 0.0090 unit. Non-institutional credit support has negative and significant coefficient. It shows that a unit increase in the amount of borrowing from non-institutional sources has reduced the output rate by 0.042 units. Non-institutional sources charge a high rate of interest and make borrowing costlier and hence this variable might have resulted in negative impact on the rate of output and statistically insignificant coefficients in the equation, on the other hand, age of the firm, training previous experience dummy for location of the firm, market extension and Entrepreneurial Behaviour Index have negative and statistically insignificant coefficients.

Credit Rate

All the 15 explanatory variables taken together have accounted for 52.6 per cent of variations in the credit rate in the multiple linear regression equation fitted for micro-enterprise model with credit rate as the dependent variable. Three variables have statistically significant coefficient in the estimated equations.

The positive and significant coefficient of the age of the firm implies that the higher the age of the firm, the higher could be the amount of credit repayment. It is quite obvious that an age old firm would be interested in protecting its reputation and good will by repaying the credit amount promptly. The coefficient of dummy variable use for inheritance has been negative and significant. The magnitude of the coefficient indicates that the credit rate of founded firms. *Cateris paribus*, has been less by 0.4241 unit than that of inherited firms. The implication is that for SHG firms, credit rate, other things remaining constant, has been less by 0.04021 unit compared to other types of organization.

Training, ancestry, dummy for location of the firm and sales have positive and statistically insignificant coefficients. In the estimated equation, capital intensity-I capital intensity-II entrepreneur's equation, age of the entrepreneur, previous experience, compensation ratio, market extension and Entrepreneurial Behaviour Index have negative and statistically insignificant coefficients.

Profit Rate

The regression equation estimated to explain the variations in the profit rate has shown a high explanatory power as the value of R^2 has been 0.91. Four variables have statistically significant coefficients in the estimated equation.

The entrepreneur's education has emerged as the most important variable influencing profit rate positively. The inference from the coefficient is that entrepreneur's education, specifically technical and professional qualification has been necessary to earn a higher return on capital. The coefficient of compensation ratio has been positive and significant. The magnitude of the coefficient implies that a unit increase in the wages of skilled workers in relation to the total wages has resulted in 0.0330 unit increase in the return on capital.

Institutional credit support has positive and significant coefficient. Its magnitude reveals that a unit increase in the credit amount from the institutional sources has helped the entrepreneur increase the profit rate by 0.0131 units. Non-institutional credit support has negative and significant coefficient. The magnitude of the coefficient points out that unit increase in the amount of borrowing from the non-institutional sources has reduced the return on capital by 0.4026 unit. The negative impact of the variable on profit rate could be attributed to the high rate of interest charged by the sources.

Capital intensity-I, age of the entrepreneur, previous experience, ancestry, dummy for location of the firm, age of the firm, market extension, Entrepreneur Behaviour Index

(EBI) and sales have positive and statistically insignificant coefficients in the equation. Capital intensity-II, training, dummy for proprietorship and dummy for inheritance have negative and statistically insignificant coefficients.

Net Profit

The estimated regression equation incorporating all the 17 explanatory variables to explain the variations in the proportion of net profit reinvested has shown a high explanatory power as the value of R^2 has been 0.945. Size variables have statistically significant coefficients in the equation.

The variable ancestry has positive and significant coefficient. It implies that entrepreneurs hailing from business communities have reinvested a larger portion of their net profit than those hailing from non-business communities. The positive and significant coefficient of entrepreneur's education shows that education, particularly technical and professional qualification has motivated entrepreneurs to plough back a higher percentage of their net profit into the same manufacturing activity for modernization and expansion.

The inference from the positive and significant coefficient of compensation ratio is that entrepreneurs who have employed more skilled workers for higher wages have been able to reinvest a higher percentage of net profit than their counterparts in micro-enterprise model. Institutional credit support has emerged as another important determinant of proportion of net profit reinvested. The positive and significant coefficient of the variable shows that micro-entrepreneurs who have availed themselves of institutional credit support is able to reinvest slightly a higher portion of their net profit for further statistically significant coefficient. However, its contribution to the variation in proportion of net profit reinvested has been negligible.

The negative and significant coefficient of non-institutional credit support points out that the amount of net profit ploughed back in micro-enterprise model declines with the increase in the non institutional credit support, previous experience, training, dummy for proprietorship, dummy for inheritance, dummy for location of the firm, EBI and sales have positive and statistically insignificant coefficients in the equation. On the other land, capital intensity-II, age of the entrepreneur, age of the firm and market extension have negative and statistically insignificant coefficients.

In micro-enterprise unit, the 'entrepreneurs' education and compensation ratio are the two variables that have positively influenced the performance of the entrepreneur measured in terms of rate of output, profit in terms of rate of output, profit rate and proportion of net profit reinvested. Non-institutional credit support has negatively affected the performance.

Employment and Income Correlation

The objectives of this section are to study the relationship between the income and employment generation of different micro-enterprises namely milch animals, vermin culture etc. The primary data were collected from individual beneficiaries of SGSY scheme in the study district. Out of these 225 beneficiaries, only 150 beneficiaries are conducting micro-enterprises. Of the several mathematical methods, correlation(r) is used to test the hypothesis that there is positive relationship between income and employment generation of the various enterprises of the SHGs. Since in <30, 't' test is used to find out the level of significance. For this purpose the above mentioned 150 beneficiaries are taken into consideration.

In the present study, the correlation methods are applied only where the deviations of items are taken from actual means and not from assumed means. The value of the coefficient of correlation 'r' always lies between –1 and +1 when $r = +1$. It means that there is perfect positive correlation between the two variables. When $r = -1$, it means that there is perfect negative correlation between the variables, when $r = 0$, it means that there is no relationship between the two variables. The coefficient of correlation described not only the magnitude of correlation but also its direction.

Given a random sample from a bivariate normal population if we are to test the hypothesis that the correlation co-efficient of the population is zero, i.e., the variables in the population are uncorrelated, we have to apply the following 't' test, since $n < 30$. It is followed by

$$\frac{r}{\sqrt{1-r^2}} \times \sqrt{n-2}$$

where, 't' is based on $(n - 2)$ degrees of freedom.

From Table 5.60, it is clear that there is positive correlation between income and employment of the beneficiaries of different enterprises of SHGs Kanyakumari district. It is inferred that the correlation is significant in the case of beneficiaries of milch animals, vermi culture, petty shops, canteen and others. The correlation is very high in the case of vermi culture and others whereas it is high in the case of the beneficiaries of milch animals and canteen. It is moderate in the case of petty shop beneficiaries.

Table 5.60. Correlation between Income and Employment Generation of Different Micro-Enterprises of SHGs

Source	'r'	Calculated 't' value	Table value at 1 % level	Table value at 5% level
Milch animals	0.7231*	5.5397	2.763	2.048
Vermiculture	0.8157*	7.4612	2.763	2.048
Petty shops	0.6215*	4.1979	2.763	2.048
Canteen	0.7212*	5.414	2.763	2.048
Others	0.8212*	7.5416	2.763	2.048

*Significant at 1 per cent level and 5 per cent level.
Source: Computed from primary data.

The vermiculture and milch animals enterprises got continuous level of employment by rearing the milch animals, goat and sheep and by collecting the waste, etc. When the continuous employment opportunities were raised due to the benefits of the SGSY programme, the income level also increased positively for the beneficiaries of the scheme.

Problems in Implementing Micro-credit Programme

Many problems crop up at the operational level in implementing a poverty alleviation programme like micro-credit. The various evaluation studies reviewed earlier highlighted the problems and issues that arose in the implementation of the programme. The basic objective of micro-finance is to lift the poor women belonging to the weaker and backward sections of the rural society above the poverty line. The women in the groups face a number of problems in getting them identified, obtaining bank loans, processing and maintaining assets, marketing products and repaying the loans. In addition to such genuine problems which they are likely to face, the women resort to malpractices, mostly out of compulsion of circumstances, such as diversion of loans to other purposes, misuse of funds, etc. The problems encountered by the SHGs and the micro-entrepreneurs in the study are analysed hereunder. The problems as reported by the respondents, is presented in Table 5.61.

The above table reveals that all the groups in the urban area (100%) and 80 per cent of groups in the rural area are facing a problem of the members being irregular in attending the group meetings. Most of the SHGs expressed the view (90%) that they had very few linkage programmes with the banks. Most of the SHGs (75% in urban, 80% in rural) are also facing the problem with inadequate training facilities and inadequate networking. Only very few groups of both urban and rural areas have mentioned that they have the problem of electing the leader of the group. The SHGs expressed the view that the members do not have much

Table 5.61. Problems faced by the Self-Help Groups in Implementing Micro-Credit Programme

Sl. No.	Problems	Respondents in Percentage	
		Urban	Rural
1.	Group conflict	60	40
2.	Inadequate bank linkage programme	90	90
3.	Inadequate networking	75	80
4.	Delay in execution of development programme	18	25
5.	Recovery of loans	17	16
6.	No training facilities	21	24
7.	General fear that the members will not make productive use of loans	60	50
8.	Members are not in regular in attending the group meeting	100	80
9.	No interest is shown by some of the members in taking decisions at the meeting	48	40
10.	Problems in electing and selecting the leader of the group	21	20

Note: Percentage given in the column relate to multiple responses evinced by the groups.

interaction during elections at the meetings. Thus the constraints expressed by the SHG members are highly relevant and realistic. The women had been dormant for many years and hence they need radical changes in their aptitude and attitude which will be a slow process. But the SHGs have made remarkable progress in upholding the sentiments and life style of women and gearing them towards positive changes.

The problems faced by the entrepreneurs in undertaking micro-enterprises is given in Table 5.62. From Table 5.62 it is clear most of the women entrepreneurs (81 per cent in urban area and 86 per cent in rural area) have expressed the view that the amount of assistance was inadequate. In

PROBLEMS FACED BY MICRO-ENTREPRENEURS

Table 5.62. Problems faced by Micro-Entrepreneurs

Sl. No.	Problems	Respondents in Percentage	
		Urban	Rural
1.	Lack of awareness of the programmes	37.19	56.39
2.	Lack of knowledge in identifying the product/trade – selection of the product and grade.	23.14	82.71
3.	Non-availability of infrastructural facilities	67.77	27.07
4.	Amount of assistance inadequate	80.99	86.47
5.	Diversion and misuse of loans	51.24	43.61
6.	Lack of training in maintaining assets and utilization of assets	56.20	47.37
7.	Inadequate supply of raw materials	19.00	33.83
8.	Inadequate marketing facilities	31.40	63.91
9.	No follow up and monitoring either by the NGO/ banks	14.88	48.87
10.	High rate of interest charged by the group	61.16	75.94
11.	Male dominance in selecting and use of assets	66.12	84.21
12.	Financial stringency	78.51	51.13
13.	Social exclusion	24.79	26.32
14.	Traditional customs recognizing the male hierarchy	21.49	58.65
15.	Gender viability to move out of their pre unit and fetch facilities	29.75	42.87
16.	Inadequate training on credit management, maintenance of books and registers, skills, upgradation, preparation of business plan	53.72	67.67

Note: Percentage given in the column relate to multiple responses tendered by the groups.

the rural area, 82.71 per cent of the members stated that they did not have much knowledge in identifying the enterprise. The rate of interest charged by the SHGs was said to be high, by as many as 61.6 per cent of the members in urban group and 75.94 per cent in the members in rural group. Diversion of loans to other purposes was resorted to in order to meet the economic exigencies arising out of personal circumstances. In the study area, it was gathered that 51.24 per cent of the members in urban groups and 43.61 per cent of the members in rural areas have misused the loans. In urban area 78.51 per cent and 51.13 per cent in rural areas have said that they are facing a problem of financial stringency, that is, interest for non-payment of interest, penalties and fines for not attending meetings and for irregular payment was imposed. It was also reported by 53.72 per cent of the women in urban area and 67.67 per cent of women in rural area that the training on credit management maintenance of books and registers, preparation of business plan, etc., was inadequate.

Appraisal of the Strengths and Weaknesses of the SHGs in Management

To examine the prospects of SHGs in micro-credit management the researcher organized an interaction meet with the members of the groups during the post-credit period. The researcher conducted two programmes one, at direct model and the other at NGO facilitated model. In each model 75 women representing 30 groups each were present. In the light of above discussion, the prospects of SHGs in micro-credit management could be broadly judged based on their strengths, weaknesses, opportunities and threats SWOT analysis was carried out on seventy five women representing all categories of the micro-enterprises initiated. SWOT analysis is a qualitative tool which by identifying the strengths, weakness, opportunities and threats to the SHGs makes an overall assessment of the performance of the groups. The responses are given in Table 5.63.

Table 5.63. Strengths and Weaknesses of the SHGs in Management and their Responses

	No. of Respondents
Strengths	
• SHGs are self-sustainable system of community organizations free from Government.	45
• Regular meetings of the group enable long lasting group relationship	64
• Groups promoted by banks and NGOs and their guidance, training to the members of the group, teaching of basic accounting principles, etc., would help for better administration of the group	25
• Social cohesion in the group and selection/election of the group leader in rotation give a sense of responsibility to each member of the group	80
• Credit portfolio covering both consumption and production purposes helps to maintain labour productivity and income generating activities	35
• No collateral securities are required at the individual level	62
• Less paper work and the sanction process is simplified	46
• Loan repayment mechanism is at the group level, hence better recovery performance	80
• Financial deepening in terms of coverage is achieved through small savers and borrowers	22
• Capacity building efforts	15
• Quick return	10
Weaknesses	
• Limited scope for future growth in membership	80
• Loan portfolio is dominated by consumption loan and hence there is limited opportunity for income generating activities	45
• Misuse and diversion of funds	65
• Higher interest rate charged by the groups	35
• Penalties and fines imposed for delay in payment	20

• Inadequate market facilities for the products	10
Opportunities	
• Women's groups exclusively dominate the SHGs, their empowerment both in economic and social fronts	70
• Opportunities for earnings through deposits and higher off farm income opportunities improve their disposable income	55
• For the banks, SHGs are better intermediaries	40
• Wide opportunity for capacity building	25
• Networking with banks, NGOs, Government departments and marketing agencies	15
• Appropriate management expertise, technology and skill training for individual and collective enterprise	52
• Exposure to the outside world	10
• Health and Social Security	35
Threats	
• SHGs do not have any legal status	55
• Rapid expansion in the number of groups without monitoring by the NGOs and banks may lead to their poor functioning	64
• Repayment failure	10
• Large number of competitors	80
• Establishing a brand and quality product is difficult	70

Social cohesion and loan repayment mechanism at the group level were considered major strengths by SHG women followed by regular meetings of the group, no requirement of collateral securities, as the next important strength. Self-sustainability, continued guidance from banks and NGOs, credit portfolio covering both consumption and production purposes, simple procedure for availing loan, capacity building efforts and quick return have been declared as cross culturally validated qualities of SHGs. Women regarding social cohesion and loan repayment mechanism at the group level as their major strength proves that these strengths gives a sense of responsibility to each member of the group and better recovery performance.

Limited scope for future growth was considered their major weakness. Misuse and diversion of funds was considered the second major weakness by the women. Loan portfolio is dominated by consumption loan and hence there is limited opportunity for income generating activities. The other weaknesses of the SHGs were, higher interest charged by the groups, penalties and fines imposed for delayed payment and inadequate market facilities for the products.

SUMMARY

The foregoing discussion reveals the profile of sample respondents of self-help groups, impact of micro-finance on self-help group members, their income generation, employment generation, consumption pattern, training status and data analysis. The data analysis reveals the correlation between employment and income, problems in implementing micro-credit programme, and strength, weakness, opportunities and threats of self-help groups in management.

REFERENCES

1. Sales has not been included in the rate of output function as it is not relevant for determining the rate of output.
2. Similarly, institutional and non-institutional credit supports have not been included in the credit rate function.
3. Heady, Earl O and Dillion, J.I., *Agricultural Function*, Loco State University Press, Aimes, 1964, p. 136.

Summary of Findings, Suggestions and Conclusion

Introduction

Credit is definitely an entry point for upliftment programmes for the rural poor. As Self-help Groups have regular transactions with banks, it is easy to extend credit to them through subsidy-linked target-oriented credit schemes like Swarnajayanthi Gram Swarozgar Yojana and Mahalir Thittam Indeed, many micro-finance programmes observe the motto "Savings First, Credit Later".

This is the approach underlying NABARD's "Linking banks with Self-help Groups" programmes, which requires the group members to save regularly, pool these savings and lend them to one another, thereby acquiring credit discipline and experience, before depositing the savings in banks as part collateral for obtaining bulk loans from the banks. It is cheaper for the banks to leave the retailing to the group, which is also responsible for collection and repayment.

Despite the vast expansion of the formal credit system in India, the dependence of the rural poor on money lenders continues in some areas, particularly for meeting urgent credit needs mainly for consumption purposes. For various reasons, the credit flow to these sections of the population for meeting their credit requirements has not been institutionalised. The credit needs of the rural poor are determined in a complex socio-economic milieu, wherein it is difficult to adopt project lending approach as followed by banks and wherein the dividing line between credit for consumption and productive purposes is blurred. In the circumstances, a non-formal agency of credit supply to the poor in the form of "Self-help Groups" of the poor could emerge as promising partner of the formal agencies. The present study attempts to analyse the impact of micro-finance on women Self-help Groups in Kanyakumari district of Tamil Nadu.

In this context, a research study was taken up to document the experience of the SHGs in promoting micro-enterprises through micro-credit interventions and evaluate the impact of the programme.

The main objective of the study is to analyse the impact of micro-finance on women SHGs Tamil Nadu.

The specific objectives of the study are:

1. To study the role of micro-finance assistance of SHGs in Kanyakumari district;
2. To analyse the performance of rural development programmes like SGSY and Mahalir Thittam through SHGs in the study district;
3. To find out the impact of the micro-finance on the women Self-help Groups in the same district;
4. To review the problems in the implementation of micro-finance activities in Tamil Nadu; and
5. To suggest the effective measures for the successful implementation of micro-finance activities through SHGs in Tamil Nadu.

Primary data as well as secondary data were used for the present study. The secondary data were collected from reports, records, books and journals relating to the performance of the SGSY scheme for a period of six years (1999-2000 to 2004-05) i.e., from the inception of the scheme upto the present. The primary data were collected from the beneficiaries of SGSY schemes in Kanyakumari district of Tamil Nadu. The Kanyakumari district is purposely selected for the study. Based on the information to be furnished by the regional office NABARD, three blocks were selected based on overall performance of the SGSY. The selected blocks are: Melpuram, Killiyoor and Kurunthencode.

There are three models of Self-Help Groups. They are: Direct linkage with banks, NGO as facilitator and NGO as intermediary. From the selected blocks 15 SHGs consist of three different models and each model represents 5 groups.

A total of 45 SHGs consist of 15 Direct linkage SHGs, 15 NGO facilitator SHGs and 15 NGO as intermediary SHGs were selected in 3 selected blocks of Kanyakumari district. Five individual Swarnogzories were identified in each group for the interview purpose. A total of 225 individual beneficiaries of SGSY scheme were interviewed with the pre tested questionnaire.

Findings

During the period of 6 years (1999-2000 to 2004-2005), the total funds allocation for the SGSY programme was Rs. 8,341.36 crore. The trend of the funds allocation shows that there is a declining trend from Rs. 1961.97 crore in 1999-2000 to 1061.22 crore in 2004-2005.

On the whole the percentage of utilization of funds available for the programme was 73.17 per cent during the six years period. The per cent of utilization of funds available was higher (86.49%) in the year 2003-2004.

The growth of credit mobilization had shown an increasing trend from Rs. 1,056.46 crore in 1999-2000 to Rs. 1,452.61 crore in 2004-2005. But the total credit disbursement of SHGs was Rs. 2,2296.49 crore.

Of the total subsidy disbursed, 1,508.43 crore (39.15 per cent) were only disbursed to the Self-help Groups under SGSY. Only Rs. 2,346 crore (60.87%) were disbursed to the individual Swarozgaries of SGSY.

The total investment under SGSY has increased from Rs. 1,598.15 crore in 1999-2000 to Rs. 1,714.01 crore in 2004-

2005. The total investment of the SGSY scheme was Rs. 11,232.15 crore during the study period. The All India target for per capita investment is Rs. 25,000. But the average per capita investment was Rs. 21,506 during the six year period.

There was a tremendous growth in the case of the SHGs involved in the economic activities. At an average, during the study period of 6 years, 44.12 per cent of the SHGs were involved in economic activities in India.

Of the total SC/ST beneficiaries, 16,32,660 (66.92%) Swarozgaries belonged to the Scheduled Caste and 807116 (33.08%) Swarozgaries belonged to the Scheduled Tribes in India. The percentage of SC/ST assisted to the total economic assistance beneficiaries was 43.86. The total women Swarozgaries assisted under SGSY during the same period was 25,38,903.

The bank loans aggregating to Rs.39,042 million were disbursed to 1,079,091 SHGs with refinance support of Rs.21,242 million from NABARD, upto 31 March 2004. Around 90 per cent of the SHGs linked were exclusive women SHGs.

The study shows that there is 8 times growth in the case of SHGs provided with bank loan during the five year period. The percentage of women groups participation has also increased from 85 to 90 per cent.

At the national level, the cooperative banks provided loan assistance to 1,34,671 SHGs for the loan amount of Rs.3,711.21 million upto 31st March 2004. In Tamil Nadu, the 24,829 SHGs got loan assistance of Rs.1,240.90 million from the cooperative banks. The commercial banks also provided loan assistance of Rs.22,548.29 million to 538.422 SHGs in India.

The Regional Rural Banks had provided loan assistance of Rs.2256.98 million to a total of 39894 SHGs in Tamil Nadu and Pondicherry. It shows 17.66 per cent and 9.83 per cent respectively of the performance as a whole of India.

The farmers and agricultural labourers are effectively involved in SHG's formation due to the seasonal occupation in the agricultural sector and the problem of unemployment.

About 65 per cent of the groups recorded more than 90 per cent of attendance during the groups meetings, which indicated the active involvement of the members.

The average savings per sample SHG during the year 2005-2006 worked out to Rs. 14,461 (Table 5.5). The savings per group was relatively higher in SHGs formed directly by the banks (Rs. 22,381).

The size of loan was observed to be relatively more in the groups formed by the banks than the other two models. The share of loans for income generating purpose was significantly higher in NGO intermediary model (91%) than NGO facilitator (63%) and direct models (65%).

The young women groups are not involved in the SGSY in the study district. The experienced middle age groups (30 to 45 years) are functioning in SGSY schemes and the SHG approach for rural development.

About 24 per cent of the sample members were illiterate and 26 per cent could sign. Members with primary education accounted for 21 per cent and those with secondary level constituted 23 per cent.

Non-farm activity constituted the major share accounting to 20 per cent, followed by farm activity (18%). Though, about 32 per cent of the sample households were agriculture labourers, only 14 per cent of them depended exclusively on agricultural labour. On the other hand, the remaining 18 per cent of them were engaged in other activities in addition to being wage earners.

Among different linkage models, the increase in assets was more in model with NGO as facilitator compared to the other two models. The proportion of households reporting increase in the assets showed positive correlation with the age of the groups.

An average SHG member household possessed assets worth Rs. 11,783 in the reference year compared to Rs. 6,843 during pre SGSY-benefits period. There was an average increase of 72.3 per cent in the assets held by members after getting the benefits of SGSY.

Interestingly, proportion of households having negligible assets (up to Rs. 1000) declined in the post-SHG situation compared to pre-SGSY situation. About one in every household was having negligible assets in pre-SGSY situation while the frequency declined to one in every six during post-SGSY situation.

Promotion of SHG situation compared to Rs. 4,282 in pre-SGSY situation, thus registering an increase of about 95 per cent. Out of this, 56 per cent was on account of borrowing by households that were not borrowing in pre SHG situation and the rest was due to increase in the quantum of borrowing per borrowing household.

SGSY accounted for about 75 per cent of the borrowed amount in the post-SGSY situation, while informal agencies like money lenders, friends and relatives, commission agents, etc., accounted for about 67.5 per cent in pre-SGSY situation.

Consumption and cultivation were two activities, which accounted for major share (77%) of loan account in the pre-SGSY situation, share of allied agricultural activities and ISB activities showed increase in the number of accounts as well as amount across all the three models.

While loans contracted at interest rates in the range of 48 to 60 per cent were insignificant in proportion to loans taken at interest rates above 60 per cent in post-SGSY situation.

Term loans of more than 36 months duration were less preferred in post-SGSY period, compared to the earlier times as indicated by the decline in their share. Their share in number and amount of loans declined from 33 and 52 per cent, respectively, in pre-SGSY period to 11 and 18 per cent, in the same order, in the post-SGSY period.

The repayment percentage among the sample households from all the sources was 94 per cent in post-SGSY situation. In general, there was not much improvement in the repayment percentage as it was already at a higher level in pre-SGSY period, the significant improvement in the repayment percentage of bank loans of the order of 29.1 per cent points notwithstanding.

In the pre-SGSY period about 36 per cent of the households were having income in the range of Rs.7500-Rs.15,000 followed by 20 per cent of the households in the range of Rs. 15,000 followed by 20 per cent of the households in the range of Rs. 15,000-Rs. 22,500. About 74 per cent of the households were having an income less than Rs. 22,500. In post-SGSY period, this proportion declined to 57 per cent indicating shift in the income distribution to higher slabs. Similar trend was observed in average loan amount also.

About 43 per cent of the incremental income generated was from NFS activities followed by farm (28%) and off-farm (21%) activities. Across all the models of linkage, NFS activities was higher compared to other activities.

The employment per household during pre-SHG situation. While 52 per cent of the employment generated was from farm activities during pre-SGSY situation, it was only 47 per cent during post-SGSY situation. On the other hand, the proportion of employment generated through non-farm and off-farm activities increased from 32 per cent and 18 per cent during pre-SGSY situation to 35 per cent and 16 per cent during post-SGSY situation, respectively.

The expenditure on food accounted for 60 per cent during pre-SGSY situation followed by clothing and festival/creation. Similar trend was observed during post-SGSY situation. However, the expenditure on food came down to 57 per cent. The per capita expenditure on food increased from Rs. 117 to Rs. 140 accounting for 20 per cent increase between pre and post-SGSY situation. Similarly, the expenditure on clothing, education, health and festivals etc., registered an increase in the post-SGSY situation.

Members option about the usefulness of the training given to them revealed that less than six per cent of the members trained felt that the training was not useful. The remaining members experienced different degrees of utility of the training with one-fourth with 73 per cent of them finding it extremely useful.

Relatively higher proportion of members (94%) under direct linkage model viewed SHGs as a source of loan compared to the other two models. Similarly, higher proportion of members under this model also felt that SHGs were helpful in capital formation. In respect of opinion on other aspects, i.e., about the group as an agent to solve social problems, as a means of elevating social status, as a link with other agencies and with banks, members of groups under models involving NGOs showed agreement more frequently compared to direct linkage model.

In pre-SGSY situation about 80 per cent of savings were made by top 10 per cent of the households. In fact, only 23 per cent of the households reported savings during this period. In post-SGSY situation, the tendency has changed and bottom 70 per cent of the households accounted for 26 per cent of the savings and the share of top ten per cent households came down to about 49 per cent. Thus, the inequality in saving pattern has come down and savings were broad based in post-SGSY situation.

Bottom 40 per cent of the households could corner 10 per cent of the credit in post-SHG situation compared to pre-SGSY situation when no credit was flowing. The share of Top 10 per cent declined from 60 per cent to 37 per cent between pre and post-SGSY situation.

The share of bottom ten per cent households in income increased from 1.4 per cent to 2.4 per cent between pre and post-SGSY periods. Share of top ten per cent households declined from 32 per cent to 29 per cent. Thus, the distribution of income was relatively less unequal in post SGSY period.

The coefficient of capital intensity has been positive and significant. It suggests that a unit increase in the fixed capital labour ratio has raised the rate of output by 0.0090 unit. The positive and significant coefficient of the age of the firm implies that the higher the age of the firm, the higher could be the amount of credit repayment. A unit increase in the credit amount from the institutional sources has helped the entrepreneur to increase the profit rate by 0.0131 units. Non-institutional credit support has negative significant coefficient. The positive significant coefficient of the variables show that micro-entrepreneurs who have availed themselves of institutional credit support were able to reinvest slightly a higher portion of their net profit for further statistically significant coefficient. However, its contribution to the variation in proportion of net profit reinvested has been negligible.

The correlation is highly significant for the beneficiaries of vermiculture enterprises. But there is low significant correlation for the Petty shop enterprises of the SHGs in the study district.

SUGGESTIONS

On the basis of the findings of the study the following suggestions have been made that would help to improve the function of the micro-credit management by the SHG members at the grass-root level:

The process of SHG formation has to be systematic, whether it is formed by a bank or an NGO. Due to their closeness to the people and flexibility of operations, the NGOs seem to be better equipped to undertake SHG formation.

The savings habit must be encouraged as a value in itself and not just as a means of increasing the fund position of the group. It encourages thrift habit and controls unnecessary consumption.

Every group needs a policy on how to manage the savings of members who leave the group voluntarily or are asked to leave for some reason.

Income generating activity should be based on available local resources and reasonably assured marked with profits. Goods to be produced, should be either for local needs or to facilitate traditional manufacture.

The NGOs should also provide some common services for procurement of raw materials, marketing/quality support.

All groups should be helped to become autonomous in their working and should have their own systems and programmes.

Institutional credit facilities must be extended to women to develop their managerial skill for prompt repayment consciousness.

Micro-credit should be used to meet the current demands of the poor women, whether these are for health, education or consumption purposes. This will lead to a gradual improvement in the quality of their life and will enable them to identify activities for economic betterment. In this process they will learn fiscal discipline and be ready to take on market oriented economic activities.

To empower women, it is necessary to make women equal partners in the national development process and equip them to make choices in order to actualise their self-worth.

Tremendous efforts are required for women's resource development in the spheres of education, health care, sanitation, food security, population education and domestic resource mobilization.

Periodic training programmes should be conducted not only for group leaders but also for the group members. To enhance the participation of all the members, exclusive membership education programmes need to be conducted.

Potential members of old groups can be motivated to take up promotional and conflict-resolution responsibilities. They can visit problematic/sick groups to explain and resolve various issues for smooth functioning.

Training in book-keeping, accounts, fund management and other financial matters related to SHGs is essential to make the members competent enough to deal with the increasing volume of transaction.

Annual Plans for SHG activities should be done by the group in consultation with the NGOs. The group leaders from different villages can meet once a month and present the progress of their groups. Such review by all the groups will promote mutual learning.

Exposure visits to relatively successful group ventures of other SHGs can be organized to share the knowledge, experience and expertise.

Rapid expansion in the number of groups should be followed by a close and continuous monitoring of their health. This is very essential to prevent the groups losing their efficacy. An effective group-monitoring system in the case of groups is a future challenge which should be met by developing group structure like clusters and federation. With the expansion of groups and its multiplier effect upon common fund, constant monitoring becomes very crucial and leaders need to be trained.

The vertical structure and their management requires capacity building and promotion of leadership from the grass-roots upwards within the SHG structure. But they should not be imposed from above.

Household surveys must be conducted in each village every year in order to identify the eligible beneficiaries of the programme and to allocate the funds according to the felt needs of the people.

The involvement of politicians in the selection of the eligible beneficiaries may be avoided. The Panchayat Raj Institution or the Grama Sabha under the New Panchayat Raj System in Tamil Nadu may be involved in selection of the beneficiaries and the nature of assistance under this programme to the people living below the poverty line.

The veterinary department should also take preventive measures and provide constant and regular guidance, timely insemination etc. For this purpose mobile veterinary units are suggested for villages to reach out to the beneficiaries' residence. This may be provided under infrastructure funds.

Government officials must take necessary action to disburse the subsidy promptly.

As suggested by Government of India, a bond should be got filled up for subsidy portion exclusively by the beneficiary to guard against misutilisation of subsidy or misappropriation of the asset.

Voluntary organization operating in the rural areas should be encouraged to participate in the effective implementation of the programme. The programme may provide separately funds for the projects to be taken by such organization.

Government should organize credit camps and credit cum-recovery camps to facilitate early completion of the formalities required for sanction of loans and to avoid hardship to the beneficiaries.

Proper infrastructure facilities should be given to the beneficiaries for effective implementation of schemes like sheep, goat, small dairy farming and other processing etc.

Banks should encourage the self-help groups who have higher savings among the group for getting the loans and subsidy.

Government should provide loan and subsidy to both male and female groups under SGSY scheme.

CONCLUSION

Careful observation has revealed that the young women groups don't directly participate in one SGSY in the study district. The functioning of SGSY schemes and the SHG approach for rural development are in evidence among the experienced middle aged groups (30-45 years). But it is a hard fact that the literate younger generations are not ready to join the SHGs. If the provisions of micro-finance is pressed into service for productive purposes instead of clearing the previous loans, there will be plenty of scope for viable income and employment generation. Once the availability of micro-finance is put to the right, productive purpose with an eye on achieving substantial results, it will pave the way for finding a solution to the problem of unemployment, ensure socio-economic development and better standard of living among the weaker sections of the community in the study area.

While concluding, it is suggested that there must be sincere efforts in creating awareness about the SGSY scheme and the importance of SHG approach especially in the backward districts like Ramanathapuram District. The success of the programme implementation depends mainly on the effective involvement of the beneficiaries and the cooperation among the implementers. The purpose of loan assistance must have the suitability of the micro-enterprises for employment generation to the weaker sections.

Bibliography

Books

Adams Dale, W., *Fitchett Informal Finance in Low Income Countries,* Westview Press, Oxford: Delbert, 1992.

Batliwala, Srilatha, "The Meaning of Empowerment New Concept from Action, I. Adrienna Germain, Gita Sen and Lincoln Chen (eds.), *Population Policies Reconsidered: Health, Empowerment and Rights,* Cambridge, Macs: Harward School of Public Health, 1994.

Bhatt, Ela, "Women and Development Alternative, Micro and Small Scale Enterprises in India" In (ed) Louise, Dignard and Jose Hennet, *Women in Micro and Small Scale Enterprise Development,* San Fransisco, Westview Press, 1997.

Calman, Leslie, J., *Towards Empowerment: Women and Movement Policies in India,* New York, Westview Press, 1992.

Carr, Marilyn, Martha Chen and Renana Jhabvala, *Speaking Out: Women's Economic Empowerment in South Asia,* New Delhi, Vistaar Publications, 1996.

Chen, Martha, A., (ed) *Beyond Credit: A Subsector Approach to Promoting Women's Enterprises,* Canada, Ottawa: Aga Khan Foundation, 1996.

Devi, Manuja, K., *Rural Women: Poverty Alleviation Programme,* New Delhi, Anmol Publications Pvt. Ltd., 1997.

Fernandez, Aloysius Prakash, *The Myrada Experience: Alternative Management Systems for Savings and Credit of the Rural Poor,* The Mysore Resettlement and Development Agency, Bangalore, 1994.

Gupta, R.C., *Management of Savings and Credit Programmes by NGOs,* New Delhi, Har-Anand Publication, 1994.

Gupta, S.P., *Statistical Methods,* New Delhi, Sultan Chand and Sons, 1996.

Gupta, Suranjana, *Visiting Alternatives on Inter State Study Tour on Savings and Credit,* Mumbai, Swamyam Shikshan Prayog, 1998.

Kamta, Prasad, (eds), *NGOs and Socio-Economic Development Opportunities,* New Delhi, Deep and Deep Publications Pvt. Ltd., 2000.

Karmakar, K.G., *Rural Credit and Self-Help Groups: Micro-Finance Needs and Concepts in India,* New Delhi, Sage Publications, 1999.

Kothari, C.R., *Research Methodology – Methods and Techniques,* New Delhi, Vishwa Prakashan, 1994.

Kuchhal, K.C., *Financial Management: An Analytical and Conceptual Approach,* Allahabad, Chaitanya Publishing House, 1999.

Kulkarni, P.V., *Financial Management – A Conceptual Approach,* New Delhi: Himalaya Publishing House, 1994.

Mullins, L.J., *Management and Organisational Behaviour,* London, Y.P. Chapra, 1992.

Narasaiah Laxmi, M., and G. Jaya Raju, *Rural Development and Anti-Poverty Programme,* New Delhi, Discovery Publishing House, 1999.

National Bank for Agriculture and Rural Development (NABARD), *International Seminar on Development of Rural Poor Through the Self-Help Groups,* Bangalore, Development Policy Department, 1996.

Pillai, J.K., *Women and Empowerment,* New Delhi, Gyan Publishing House, 1995.

Quinones, Benjamin, R., *Self-Help Groups as Informal Financial Intermediaries,* Bangkok, Asia Pacific Rural and Agricultural Credit Association, 1992.

Rhona, Howarth and Longdon Karen, *Organising Self-Help Groups,* New Delhi, Department of Women and Child Development, 2000.

Ridgeway, C.L., *The Dynamics of Small Groups,* New York, Martin Press, 1983.

Sahay, Sushma, *Women and Empowerment: Approaches and Strategies,* New Delhi, Discovery Publishing House, 1998.

Sekaran, Uma, *Organisation Behaviour: Text and Cases,* New Delhi, Tata McGraw Hill Publishing Company Limited, 1994.

Sen, Biswaji, *From Self-Help Groups to Community Banking,* The Pradhan Project for Empowerment of Women and Resource Centre, Bangalore, 1997.

Sinha, Tara, *Net Work of Self-Help Groups,* New Delhi, Department of Women and Child Development, 2000.

Srinivasan, Girija, *Training of Self-Help Groups,* New Delhi Micro-credit Development Bureau, 2000.

Subramanian, K., and T.K. Velayudham, (eds), *Banking Reforms in India – Managing Change,* New Delhi, Tata McGraw Hill Publishing Company Limited, 1997.

Wilkinson, T.S., and Bhadarkar, P.L., *Methodology and Techniques of Social Research,* Mumbai, Himalaya Publishing House, 1982.

Young, K., *Gender and Development: A Rational Approach,* London, Oxford University, 1988.

Journals

Arora, Sukhwaider Singh and Mankad, Dhurv, "Banking on the Poor", *National Bank News Review*, Vol. 11, No. 2, April-June 1995.

Besley, T., and S. Coate, "Group Lending, Repayment Incentives and Social Collateral", *Journal of Development Economics*, Vol.46, No.1, 1995.

Bhagalakshmi, "Environment of Women through Thrift and Credit Groups", *Gramvikas Newsletter*, Vol. 11, No. 3, June 1995.

Bhatt, Ela, R., "Micro-Insurance is Micro-Finance", *The Economics Times*, July 31, Mumbai.

Desai, B.M., "Review of Book: A Study of SHGs and Linkage Programme", *Indian Journal of Agricultural Economics*, Vol.55, No.1, January-March 2000.

Goetz, A.M., and R. Sen Gupta, "Who Takes the Credit?, Gender, Power and Control over loan use in Rural Credit Programmes in Bangladesh", *World Development*, Vol. 24, No. 1, 1996.

Gopalan Sarala, "Paradigm Shift from Welfare to Empowerment", *Social Welfare*, Vol.43, No.5, 1996.

Hans, Dieter Siebel, "Agricultural Development Banks Close them on Reform them", *Finance and Development,* Washington, D.C.: International Monetary Fund, 2000.

Ilanto, Gilerto, M., "Asymmetric Information in Rural Financial Markets and Interlinking of Transactions through the Self-Help Groups", *Savings and Development*, Vol. 14, No. 2, 1990.

Jain, R.K., "Economics Self-Reliance for Women", *Social Welfare*, Vol. XI, No. 11-12, 1994.

Kausik, Amarchand, "Income Generations Effects of Rural Credit: A Case Study of IRDP in Haryana", *Journal of Rural Development*, Vol. 12, No. 1, 1993.

Khalkar, R.K., "Impact of IRDP on Income, Employment and Consumption Expenditure of Rural Poor in Mahendragarh District of Haryana State", *Journal of Rural Development*, Vol. 6, No. 5, 1987.

Koch, Eckart, "Linking Banks and Self-Help Groups in Indonesia Experiences and Strategies", *Asia Pacific Rural Finance*, Vol. 5, No. 3, January-March 1993.

Krishnaveni, L., and Sujma, A.L., "Women's Status – Does Employment Enhance Decision Making Power?", *Social Welfare*, Vol. 39, No. 9, 1992.

Kumaran, "Self-Help Groups: An Alternative to Institutional Credit to the Poor: A Case Study in Andhra Pradesh", *Journal of Rural Development*, Vol. 16, No. 3, 1997.

Lalitha, N., "Women's Empowerment through Co-operatives", *Social Welfare*, Vol. 43, No. 6, 1996.

Manivannan, R., "Innovations in Rural Lending: Self-Help Groups", *Indian Overseas Bank Monthly News Review*, Vol. 5, No. 6, June 1992.

Misra, A., "Self-Help Programme", *Tamilarasu*, Government of Tamil Nadu, 1997.

Misra, B., "Approach to the Ninth Plan: Need for Hard Decisions", *Kurukshetra*, Vol. XLV, 1997.

Mohan, R., "Major Revamp of Banking System Urge", *Business Line*, September 27, 1997.

Montogomery, Richard, "Discipline or Protecting the Poor? Avoiding the Social costs of Peer Group Pressure in Micro-credit Schemes", *Journal of International Development*, Vol. 8, No. 2, 1996.

Parvathi, S., Chandrakandan, K., Ganeshan, R., and C. Sekhar, "Economic Empowerment Needed", *Social Welfare*, Vol. 43, No. 1, 1996.

Pathak, P.A., "Self-Help Groups and their Linkages with Banks", *National Bank News Review*, Vol. 7, No. II, 1992.

Paul, B., McGuire and d. John, "Conory Bank – NGO Linkages and the Transaction Costs of Lending to the Poor through Groups", *National Bank News Review*, October-December 1997.

Pramod, B., "Developing Banking for the Poor : A Conceptual Framework", *Pigmy Economic Review*, Vol. 35, No. II, June 1990.

Prasad, Hemalatha, C., and Prakashom, "Sustainable Employment for Women, Mahila Chetna Manch Shows the Way *Grameen Vikas Newsletter*, June 1997.

Rajasekar, D., "Problems and Prospects of Group Lending in NGO Credit Programme in India", *Savings and Development*, Vol. 20, No. 1, 1996.

Rangarajan, C., "Banking with the Poor", *Reserve Bank of India Bulletin*, Vol. XLVIII, No. 2, February 1994.

Rangarajan, V., "Rural Banking – Lesson from the Past", *National Bank News Review*, July-September 1995.

Shridharan, Damyanty, "Encourage Self-Help Group", *Social Welfare*, Vol. 44, No. 7, October 1997.

Srinivasan, Girija, "Reaching Credit to Rural Poor – I: Legal Hurdles on the Path of Self-Help Groups", *Business Line*, January 31, 1996.

Srinivasan, Girija, "Reaching Credit to Rural Poor – II: Legal Hurdles on the Path of Self-Help Groups", *Business Line*, January 31, 1996.

Stigliz, J.E., "Peer Monitoring and Credit Markets", *The World Bank Economic Review*, Vol. 4, No. 3, 1990.

Sudheer, G., "Small Group Approach", *Kurukshetra*, Vol. XLN, No. 3, December 12.

Sundaram, Rao, S., and G. Padmaja, "Self-Help Groups in Tirupati", *Social Welfare*, Vol. 45, No. 1, April 1998.

Vasimalai, M.P., "Community Banking: Kalanjiam Way", *National Bank News Review*, Vol. 11, No. 4, October-December 1995.

Veni, K.L., "Status of India Women", *Social Welfare*, Vol. 43, No. 10, 1997.

Viswanathan, Sujatha, "Grouping Women for Economic Empowerment", *Yojana*, Vol. XII, No. 6, March 1997.

Yadav, A., Sangwan, V., Yadav, B.L., and S. Gandhi, "Potential and Preference of Rural Women for Income Generating Activities", *Khadi Gramodyog*, Vol. 41, No. 11, August 1995.

Zelle, M., "Determinants of Repayment Performance in Credit Groups: The Role of Programme Design, Intra-Group Risk Polling and Social Cohesion", *Economic Development and Cultural Change*, Vol. 46, April 1998.

Reports

Brochure of The Indonesian Movement for Micro-Finance Development, Indonesia, A Network of Indonesia Micro-Finance Actors for Poverty Alleviation, 2000.

Brochures of NABARD, *Emerging Micro-Finance Innovations*, New Delhi, 1997.

Cheston, Susy, Larry Reed, *Measuring Transformation: Assessing and Improving the Impact of Micro-credit*, Paper presented at the Micro-Credit Summit Meeting of Councils in Abidjan, Coted' Ivoire: 24-26, June.

Das, Maitrcyi, *The Women's Development Programme in Rajasthan: A Case Study in Group Formation for Women's Development*, Population and Human Resource Department, The World Bank, 1991.

Department of Women and Child Development, *Annual Report*,

Part-IV, New Delhi, 1996.

Department of Women and Child Development, *Fourth World Conference on Women*, Country Paper, 1994, Beijing, New Delhi, 1995.

Department of Women and Child Development, *Rashtriya Mahila Kosh: A Profile and Operational Guidelines*, New Delhi, 1996.

Department of Women and Child Development, *Rashtriya Mahila Kosh: Features of the Maina and Sub-Schemes*, New Delhi, 1996.

Department of Women and Child Development, *Workshop on Best Practices in Group Dynamics and Micro-Credit*, New Delhi, February 15-17, 2000.

Gibbons David, S., *The Micro-Credit Summits Challenge Working Towards Institutional Financial Self-sufficiency while Maintaining a Commitment to Serving the Poorest Families*, Paper presented at Micro-Credit Summit Meeting of Councils in Abidjasi Coted' Ivoire, June 1999.

Grameen Connections, *The Newsletter of Grameen Foundation*, Vol.4, Issue No.1, USA: 2000-2001.

Grameen Vikas Newsletter, Ushering in a new Era of Women's Empowerment, New Delhi, Vol. 13, No. 4, 1997.

International Fund for Agriculture and Development Policy on Rural Finance (IFAD), June 2000.

National Bank for Agriculture and Rural Development (NABARD), *Studies on Self-Help Groups of the Rural Poor*, Mumbai, 1989.

National Institute of Bank Management, *Workshop on Linkages Between Self-Help Group and financing Institution*, Pune, 1991.

Proceedings of First Meeting, *Indian Collective for Micro-Finance*, New Delhi, 3-4 December 1997.

Rashtriya Mahila Kosh, *Annual Report*, New Delhi, 1995.

Reserve Bank of India, *Report of Trend and Progress of Banking in India*, 1997-98.

Sen, Biswajit, *From Self-Help Groups to Community Banking*, Bangalore, The Pradhan Project for Empowerment of Women and Resource Centre, 1997.

The Hindu, Community Banking by Rural Women a Hit, September 20, 1998.

The Indian Express, Fatima B. *Selected for UNDP's Race Against Poverty Award*, Vol.LXVI, October 3, 1998.

United Nations Development Programme (UNDP), Annual Report, *Enduing Poverty and Building Peace through Sustainable Human Development*, New York, 1996-97.

United Nations Development Programme (UNDP), *The Human Development Report*, New York, Oxford University, 1995.

United Nations, *The World's Women: Trends and Statistics*, New York, 1995.

Zeller, Manfrad and Manohar Sharma, *Rural Finance and Poverty Alleviation*, Food Policy Report, International Food Policy Research Institute, Washington, D.C., 1998.

Index